MySQL and JSON
A Practical Programming Guide

About the Author

Dave Stokes started programming in FORTRAN on punch cards. Decades ago, he found an open-source database named MySQL. He formerly was a PHP programmer in the MySQL AB Certification Department and eventually was the MySQL Certification Manager for MySQL AB, Sun Microsystems, and Oracle. He has been a member of the MySQL Community Team for Oracle. His professional background includes organizations, ranging alphabetically, from the American Heart Association to Xerox and in areas ranging from anti-submarine warfare to web development.

About the Technical Editor

After graduating in Management Information Technology, **Frédéric Descamps** (@lefred) started his career as a developer for an ERP under HPUX. He then opted for a career in the world of open source by joining one of the first Belgian startups dedicated 100 percent to free projects around GNU/Linux. In 2011, Frédéric joined Percona, one of the leading MySQL-based specialists. He decided to join the MySQL Community Team in 2016 as a MySQL Community Manager for EMEA and APAC. His blog, which is mostly dedicated to MySQL, is at lefred.be.

Oracle Press™

MySQL and JSON
A Practical Programming Guide

David Stokes

New York   Chicago   San Francisco
Athens   London   Madrid   Mexico City
Milan   New Delhi   Singapore   Sydney   Toronto

Cataloging-in-Publication Data is on file with the Library of Congress

McGraw-Hill Education books are available at special quantity discounts to use as premiums and sales promotions, or for use in corporate training programs. To contact a representative, please visit the Contact Us pages at www.mhprofessional.com.

MySQL and JSON: A Practical Programming Guide

1 2 3 4 5 6 7 8 9 QFR 21 20 19 18

ISBN   978-1-260-13544-2
MHID   1-260-13544-6

Sponsoring Editor Lisa McClain	**Acquisitions Coordinator** Claire Yee	**Indexer** Karin Arrigoni
Editorial Supervisor Janet Walden	**Technical Editor** Frédéric Descamps	**Production Supervisor** James Kussow
Project Manager Smriti Joinwal, Cenveo® Publisher Services	**Copy Editor** Lisa Theobald **Proofreader** Lisa McCoy	**Composition** Cenveo Publisher Services **Art Director, Cover** Jeff Weeks

*This book is dedicated to my long-suffering wife, Carrie Stokes.
In 2017, I rode more than 85,000 miles on American Airlines alone and was
gone to too many conferences. And then when I get home I started spending
more time closed away in my office to finish this book! She put up with
a lot for my career and for this book and deserves a big thanks.*

CONTENTS

ACKNOWLEDGMENTS

To my coworkers—I joined MySQL as a PHP programmer in the Certification Division in 2007 after using the database for many years. Every MySQL-er has impressed me greatly, and I regularly feel like the dim bulb in a sea of shining neon lasers when we get together. To say MySQL has grown and thrived through the efforts of many persons is an understatement, and I am frankly humbled (and surprised) to be around you all.

To the MySQL Community—I am routinely set to slack-jaw yokel mode when talking to members of the MySQL Community when they tell me what they are doing with this incredible database. You folks routinely come up with new ways and combinations of using MySQL that impress me.

To Lisa McClain and Claire Yee at McGraw-Hill Education—Lisa did not laugh when I sent in pages of the early stages of this book, and both have guided me through the process of getting this book published.

1
Introduction

Once upon a time, there was one computer. With the creation of a second computer, we experienced problems moving and sharing data between systems. It took decades of hard work, arguments, negotiations, and proposed standards, and a great deal of frustration, to get to the point where data transfer between systems is almost trivial. For many years, many very smart people argued over ASCII or EBCDIC character encoding, endianness of computer memory, and various standards such as the Standard Generalized Markup Language (SGML) and the Extensible Markup Language (XML). Today, JavaScript Object Notation, or JSON, has become the favorite way to encode data for moving between various systems. JSON-encoded data has several advantages over previous efforts in that it is very human-readable, easy to parse with programs, and not overly complicated.

Considering the vast increase in the volume of data being shared every year, it is imperative that the information be shared in an easy-to-digest format. Having an easy-to-produce format provides benefits like ease of programming, ease of proofreading or debugging, and low cost of entry. JSON provides these benefits beautifully.

MySQL had more than 20 years of life before it received a native JSON data type. So as with an INTEGER, a DECIMAL, or a DATE data type, we can store an entire JSON document in a column of a row of a schema. MySQL 5.7 arrived with the ability to store roughly a gigabyte of data in a column in a row in a table. Before the native JSON data type, there were special schemas or user-defined functions with limited JSON support. This new data type has proven to be very popular and has probably encouraged many site administrators to upgrade from much earlier versions of MySQL to gain access to it.

JSON

JavaScript Object Notation (JSON) is a text-based, language-independent data interchange format for the serialization of data. It is derived from the object literals of JavaScript as defined in the third edition of the *ECMAScript Language Specification*. There are actually two standards for JSON: Internet Engineering Task Force (IETF) Request For Comment (RFC) 7159 (https://tools .ietf.org/html/rfc7159) and the European Computer Manufacturers Association (ECMA) Standard 404 (https://www.ecma-international.org/publications/standards/Ecma-404.htm). The IETF's document is about 16 pages long, while ECMA's is 5. This is a relatively short set of standards compared to the IETF RFC 5321 for the Simple Mail Transfer Protocol (SMTP) at 95 pages. But the two standards for JSON are fairly explicit.

JSON has a grammar, and it is simple. JSON is a series of tokens: six structural characters ([,], {, }, :, and ,), strings, numbers, and three literal names (false, null, or true). Objects begin and end with curly brackets, { and }, respectively; arrays begin and end with square brackets, [and], respectively. A colon (:) is used to separate a name and a value. Multiple objects or arrays are separated by commas (,). Like toy building blocks, simple components can be combined to create much more complex structures.

Although I have described the attributes, it may be easier to think of JSON data being structured as objects with name/value pairs or as ordered lists of values, also known as arrays. Most programming languages and their programmers use objects and/or arrays on a regular basis. The simple design of JSON enables it to be independent of the computer language used to generate or read the data.

So what does JSON look like? Here's a simple example:

Example 1-1   *Example of a JSON document*

```
{
    "name"  :  "Bond",
    "first":  "James",
    "ID"    :  "007"
}
```

The data is enclosed within curly braces, which tells us it is a JSON object, rather than an array, which would have the data within square brackets. Inside this object are three key/value pairs: name/Bond, first/James, and ID/007. Although all of the data could have been placed on one line and would still be a valid JSON document, it is formatted as multiple lines for ease of reading. For now, you can consider all the keys and their values as *strings*.

UTF8MB4 Character Set

The JSON specifications mandate the use of the UTF8MB4 character set. This character set allows the encoding of many languages, graphics, and emoji. Note that UTF8MB4 is a 4-bit character set, which means this data will take up four times as much space as data in a simpler character set such as Latin-1. In some cases, this inefficiency may preclude the use of the JSON data type, despite its rich ability to store a wide variety of data.

MySQL

This is not a book on administrating, programming, or using MySQL. To use the information in this book, however, you will need access to a server running MySQL 5.7.5 or later, on a local system or system available over a network. The Community Edition of the MySQL server is free and available for Microsoft Windows, Linux, and Mac OS; or it's available as source code. There is a paid Enterprise Edition for customers with support contracts, and the examples included herein will also work with this edition.

If you need to install MySQL, follow the directions at the MySQL Documentation site: https://dev.mysql.com/doc/. Follow the instructions appropriate for your operating system platform. You can also install MySQL within a virtualized server or container for the purposes of this book. Remember that you need at least MySQL 5.7 or 8.0 to have access to the MySQL functions.

Be aware that Oracle engineers who create and maintain the MySQL software have evolved the way JSON and the JSON functions work as the standards have changed, as users have given feedback on the product, and as part of general improvements in the product. Hopefully, all these changes are noted in the text, but be aware that the version of MySQL you are running may behave slightly differently from previous or later versions.

The Example Database

The examples in this book will mainly use the world_x example dataset or are short enough to easily be retyped by the reader. The predecessor, world database, has been used for many years by MySQL in documentation, training, examples, and blogs. After installing the latest and greatest MySQL version, you can install the world_x database after downloading it from https://dev.mysql.com/doc/index-other.html.

You can perform the installation in several ways, but the most popular two ways are from a command line and from within the MySQL shell. There are other methods as well, but these two are very reliable and simple. Following are examples.

Example 1-2   *Installing the world_x database from the Linux shell*

```
shell> mysqlsh -u root --sql --recreate-schema world_x < /tmp/world_x-db/
world_x.sql
```

Example 1-3   *Installing the world_x database from the MySQL shell*

```
Connect to MySQL:
    shell> mysql -u root -p
Load the file:
    mysql> SOURCE /tmp/world_x-db/world_x.sql;
```

NOTE   *In some cases, the schema may not be created already, and it will report an error. This is easy to fix, and you can re-create the schema with*

```
mysqlsh -u root --sql --recreate-schema --schema=world_x < world_x.sql
```

How to Use This Book

This book was designed for readers to enter the examples on their own installations of MySQL. Some people can learn very efficiently by just reading, but many more gain additional insight by typing the examples into their own MySQL instance. The simple examples that follow can easily be deleted later when no longer needed.

The official MySQL software documentation is the definitive reference on the various features of MySQL. However, the examples in the documentation are often hard to grasp for novices at the start of the learning curve or for the experienced but not in a certain facet. So use this book to backfill areas where the manual is nebulous, confusing, or just not at your level.

Some points, such as array numbering starting at zero and document pathing, are restated over and over again and may seem tiresome and pedantic for those reading from the first page through to the last. But many readers will use this book by referring only to the part of a section that concerns them at the moment. Those folks may be oblivious to warnings presented a page or more earlier, and being dogmatic on these points will save those people grief.

One of the problems in learning computer technologies is learning to understand mistakes. This includes learning to understand error messages and warnings. If you make a mistake in entering one of the examples, examine any messages for clues and then compare what has been entered with what is in this text. It's quite common to miss a single or double quote and transpose keywords when entering SQL, but the server will not simply tell you that you fat-fingered a code entry. So you must learn to comprehend the error messages to find out where you have goofed. *Do not be afraid to make mistakes!* Mistakes are part of learning, and learning to fix mistakes is part of the process. Many martial arts experts stress that the difference between a novice and a master is that a master knows when a mistake is starting and can rectify it before it becomes a problem. Rectifying fat-fingered commands is a regular occurrence and a great way for you to learn to understand what error messages are trying to tell you.

It is very hard for a static item, like this book, to keep current with ever-changing software. Some of the functions discussed herein have evolved over time, and some are in an experimental, evolving stage. Please use this book as an addendum to the official MySQL software documentation. I have tried to make this book as useful as possible, but as time marches on, the details inside may not reflect the actual software—and that is actually a good thing.

This book starts with "once upon a time," and I would like to have it end with "they lived happily ever after." The engineers at MySQL and contributors from the MySQL Community have put a lot of effort into the JSON data type and the supporting functions. New uses such as the MySQL Document Store will hopefully bring new changes. JSON and MySQL combine to make a lot of things very convenient for developers, and the future should only improve, thus allowing all involved to live happily ever after.

Finally, any errors or omissions are my own, and I take full responsibility for them.

2

JSON as String Data vs. JSON as a Data Type

Developers were using JSON in MySQL long before there was a MySQL JSON data type in version 5.7. There is nothing special about JSON that keeps it from being used in earlier versions of MySQL, and there are cases where not using the MySQL data type is preferred. This may seem confusing or contradictory but all will be explained later in this chapter.

JSON String Data

In versions of MySQL released before version 5.7, developers were storing JSON in MySQL in text fields (such as CHAR, VARCHAR, TEXT, or BLOB). And this remains a viable option for developers running versions of MySQL prior to version 5.7.

Example 2-1 *JSON stored as a string*

```
mysql> CREATE TABLE foo (oldJson char(250));
Query OK, 0 rows affected (0.32 sec)

mysql> INSERT INTO foo VALUES ('{ "name" : "Bond", "first" : "James", "ID" :
"007" }');
Query OK, 1 row affected (0.04 sec)

mysql> SELECT * FROM foo;
+-------------------------------------------------------+
| oldJson                                               |
+-------------------------------------------------------+
| { "name" : "Bond", "first" : "James", "ID" : "007" }  |
+-------------------------------------------------------+
1 row in set (0.00 sec)

mysql>
```

This method enables JSON data to be stored. Basically, MySQL stores a string, and nothing is done to validate that it is a valid JSON document. Nothing is done to enforce rigor on the data to ensure that the correct type of data or value range is being inserted. There is no way to ensure that the tags are consistent, and it can be painful to search. For instance, a field for e-mail may be labeled email, eMail, electronic-mail, or one of dozens of other variations. The ability to examine textual JSON information lies with various string functions in MySQL or other programming languages, which are often cumbersome to search.

One benefit of keeping JSON data in a string, however, is that the data will come out as it was put in—this is known as *impotency*. Later in this chapter, you'll see that the native MySQL JSON data type "optimizes" the data and sorts the keys in the key/value pairs so that the native JSON data type does not ensure impotency. If exact regurgitation of the data is needed, then the JSON data type should not be used.

Searching can be done using *regular expressions* (REGEX). Regular expressions are often messy, hard to document, and even harder to understand. Many developers avoid them at all costs, but that is a bit extreme. It is not uncommon to fail to comprehend your own REGEX code written weeks or months before. Here's an example of REGEX code used in a SELECT query:

Example 2-2 *Using a REGEX in a SELECT query*

```
mysql>  SELECT * FROM foo WHERE oldJson REGEXP 'Bond';
+-------------------------------------------------------------+
| oldJson                                                     |
+-------------------------------------------------------------+
| { "name" : "Bond", "first" : "James", "ID" : "007" }        |
+-------------------------------------------------------------+
1 row in set (0.00 sec)

mysql>
```

Many developers are very good at writing regular expressions, but many more are not. Often regular expressions are easy to overcomplicate and painful to debug. Take the following example, in which the entire first name of the person to search for is not exactly known, so the search is written to look for a Jim, Jam, or James using a wildcard character (*):

Example 2-3 *For an experiment, change 'j*m' to 'Fred' to observe the message for no matches.*

```
mysql> SELECT * FROM foo WHERE oldJson REGEXP 'J*m';
+-------------------------------------------------------------+
| oldJson                                                     |
+-------------------------------------------------------------+
| { "name" : "Bond", "first" : "James", "ID" : "007" }        |
+-------------------------------------------------------------+
1 row in set (0.00 sec)
```

This example worked because a record was found. But suppose the searcher could not remember whether the name was Jim, James, Robert, or Lynn. The regular expression could be rewritten to search for these variables, but it gets much more difficult to interpret. And it's more difficult to maintain.

Indexing columns to speed searches is common, popular, and highly encouraged under the right circumstances. Indexing an entire text column (but not BLOBs) can be done in most circumstances, but, once again, REGEX has to be used for searching. And the indexes could end up bigger than the data, which would remove any speed advantage to having an index. So do not index blobs including JSON data type columns.

Any changes in the data require that you completely rewrite the string into the database, instead of writing only the changes, which is far more efficient. Early editions of the MySQL 5.7 functions did complete rewrites of JSON data type fields, but the engineers quickly sought to go the more efficient route.

The JSON Data Type

MySQL 5.7 introduced a JSON data type. This means that JSON is a data type, just like INT, REAL, CHAR, VARCHAR, or BLOB. The JSON data type is designed to hold valid JSON documents. Here's an example:

Example 2-4   *Using the JSON data type*

```
mysql> CREATE TABLE bar (our_data JSON);
Query OK, 0 rows affected (0.40 sec)
mysql> INSERT INTO bar VALUE ('{ "name" : "Bond",
"first" : "James", "ID" :
 "007" }');
```

The insertion string is the same as the one used in the first example in the chapter, where the data was stored in a CHAR(250) column.

Example 2-5   *Selecting JSON data from a JSON data type column*

```
mysql> SELECT * FROM bar;
+----------------------------------------------------+
| our_data                                           |
+----------------------------------------------------+
| {"ID": "007", "name": "Bond", "first": "James"}    |
+----------------------------------------------------+
1 row in set (0.00 sec)

mysql>
```

Notice the order of the returned data. The ID column is now first instead of last, as it was in the preceding example. The MySQL server stores JSON data in a binary format optimized for quick searches, which may cause the keys to be returned in an order different from how they were entered. Why is this?

The server first checks to ensure that the document is in a valid JSON format. (If it's not, the server will return an error.) Then the data is stored in a special internal format optimized for quick lookup by keys or array index position. Think of it as similar to a B-tree or B+-tree, as used by MySQL for indexes within a binary search, when the keys have to be set up in alphabetical order to allow for fast binary-style searches to retrieve the data. The order of the keys may change when the data is stored.

3
Finding the Path

The server checks to make sure this data bound for the JSON data type column is in a valid JSON format and organizes the data for faster searching. The document is divided up into *keys* and *values*, and values can also comprise a deeper set of keys and values. These various keys and values are divided into the component parts and provide the way, or path, to navigate through the document. Much of MySQL's JSON path expression work was heavily influenced by Facebook's DocStore project.

The JSON document is made up of key/value pairs, arrays, and/or possibly combinations of the previous. These items that make up the document need a path to get to the value. This can be a named key or a positional representation ($[1]). Some documents can get quite complicated, but this chapter will use a fairly simple dataset and its JSON formatted data.

Several of the MySQL-supplied JSON functions require a path expression in order to specify unique elements in a JSON document. A *path* consists of the scope of the path (the outer curly or square brackets), followed by one or more path legs made up of the key/value pairs. The MySQL JSON functions are built with the idea that the scope is always the document being searched or otherwise operated on, represented by a leading $ character. Path legs are separated using period characters (.). Cells in arrays are represented by [*N*], where *N* is a non-negative integer (so *N* must be zero or larger). The names of keys must be strings enclosed in double quotes.

Examining the world_x Data

MySQL documentation, instructional materials, and other materials have used the world database for a long time. The world_x database was created from the data in the world database for use with the document store and X DevAPI materials for the same purpose. It also offers a very good set of data for showing the use of MySQL's JSON functions. The city, country, and countrylanguages tables are the same in both databases, but world_x has a new table named countryinfo. Chapter 11 provides an introduction to the MySQL document store, which is built on the MySQL JSON data type, and the countryinfo table is an example of a document collection used to teach the MySQL document store.

The countryinfo table has two columns, with one being of data type JSON. I'll discuss the second column in Chapter 7, which covers generated columns. (These two columns will make a little more sense later in Chapters 11 and 12. For now, please concentrate on the JSON column named doc. Note that this name will be used over and over again for JSON columns and hopefully this will not cause confusion—and you can name JSON columns something else at your discretion.)

Examining one record, in the following example, the record with the _id field equal to USA returns one example record. Since it is all enclosed in curly brackets, it is obvious that the output is a JSON object.

Example 3-1   *Selecting one record from the countryinfo collections, using the _id of USA*

```
mysql> SELECT doc FROM countryinfo WHERE _id='USA';
| doc
| {"GNP": 8510700, "_id": "USA", "Name": "United States", "IndepYear": 1776,
 "geography": {"Region": "North America", "Continent": "North America",
 "SurfaceArea": 9363520}, "government": {"HeadOfState": "George W. Bush",
 "GovernmentForm": "Federal Republic"}, "demographics": {"Population":
 278357000, "LifeExpectancy": 77.0999984741211}} |

1 row in set (0.00 sec)

mysql>
```

You can read the various items in Example 3-1, but it is difficult to see the levels and relationships. Luckily, there is a function to improve readability:

Example 3-2   *Using the JSON_PRETTY function*

```
mysql> SELECT JSON_PRETTY(doc) FROM countryinfo WHERE _id='USA';
| {
  "GNP": 8510700,
  "_id": "USA",
  "Name": "United States",
  "IndepYear": 1776,
  "geography": {
    "Region": "North America",
    "Continent": "North America",
    "SurfaceArea": 9363520
  },
  "government": {
    "HeadOfState": "George W. Bush",
    "GovernmentForm": "Federal Republic"
  },
  "demographics": {
    "Population": 278357000,
    "LifeExpectancy": 77.0999984741211
  }
} |
```

The JSON_PRETTY() function was introduced with MySQL 8 (and back-ported into MySQL 5.7.22) and is used to improve readability of the output. It is similar to pretty printing used in PHP and other programming languages. It displays each element on its own line and indents it in an additional level from the parent. Two spaces are prepended for each level of indentation, and note that a comma is printed before a newline separating elements.

In addition to cleaning up the output, JSON_PRETTY() provides the casual observer an easier-to-understand view of the data. It becomes easier to examine the data—objects and arrays—and see the structure, and it's much easier to see the keys, values, and path and how they are arranged.

NOTE   *You may have noticed who is listed as HeadOfState in the previous examples. Although the data in the dataset is notoriously out of date, the examples remain valid!*

Seeing the Keys

You can use another function, JSON_KEYS(), to display the individual keys:

Example 3-3   *Using the JSON_KEYS function*

```
mysql> SELECT JSON_KEYS(doc) FROM countryinfo WHERE _id='USA';
+----------------------------------------------------------------------------+
| JSON_KEYS(doc)                                                             
|                                                                            |
+----------------------------------------------------------------------------+
| ["GNP", "_id", "Name", "IndepYear", "geography", "government", "demographics"] |
+----------------------------------------------------------------------------+
1 row in set (0.00 sec)

mysql>
```

If you are using MySQL8, you can also wrap JSON_PRETTY() around JSON_KEYS() to improve readability. Generally, you can wrap one function within other functions, but it is advisable that you double-check your work to ensure that the combination makes logical sense—that is, that you are not trying to aggregate arrays of objects—and produces the desired results correctly.

In the following example, note that only the top-level keys are being displayed. So geography is displayed, but not the subitems of Region, Continent, and SurfaceArea:

Example 3-4   *Using JSON_PRETTY and JSON_KEYS together*

```
mysql> SELECT JSON_PRETTY(JSON_KEYS(doc)) FROM countryinfo WHERE _id='USA';
| JSON_PRETTY(JSON_KEYS(doc))                                                
|                                                                            |
| [
  "GNP",
```

```
    "_id",
    "Name",
    "IndepYear",
    "geography",
    "government",
    "demographics"
]  |
1 row in set (0.00 sec)
```

Path

To get the geography information, we need to specify the path. After naming the column, a second argument for the path to search is under the top level. Using the dollar sign ($) to represent the current document (remember the JSON column is a JSON document), you can specify the keys under the geography key:

Example 3-5   *Selecting second-level keys*

```
mysql> SELECT JSON_KEYS(doc,"$.geography") FROM countryinfo WHERE _id='USA';
+----------------------------------------+
| JSON_KEYS(doc,"$.geography")           |
+----------------------------------------+
| ["Region", "Continent", "SurfaceArea"] |
+----------------------------------------+
1 row in set (0.00 sec)

mysql>
```

Note that JSON_KEYS(doc, "$") returns the top-level keys. The second through *n*th level keys must be post-pended to the $.

Digging Deeper

How can you dig down further in the document to get more information? First, the *scope* of what the function is acting on is the current document, also known as $. The path is made up of one or more legs in the document. These legs can comprise arrays and objects, the keys and values. To get all the information stored with the geography key, then, you need to specify "$.geography". This will provide all the key/value pairs under the geography subpath for this document.

Example 3-6 *Digging into second-level keys*

```
mysql> SELECT JSON_EXTRACT(doc,"$.geography") FROM countryinfo WHERE _id='USA';
+---------------------------------------------------------------------------------+
| JSON_EXTRACT(doc,"$.geography")
|
+---------------------------------------------------------------------------------+
| {"Region": "North America", "Continent": "North America", "SurfaceArea": 9363520} |
+---------------------------------------------------------------------------------+
```

But what if you needed to go further down the `geography` subpath? For instance, what if the `Region` section of the subpath is the desired information? Then you'd need to specify the subpath and the key of the desired pair. In Example 3-7, the full path `$.geography.Region` is provided to retrieve the desired information. And, yes, it is case-sensitive.

Example 3-7 *Digging deeper using the keys to explore the geography.Region values*

```
mysql> SELECT JSON_EXTRACT(doc,"$.geography.Region") FROM countryinfo WHERE _id='USA';
+--------------------------------------+
| JSON_EXTRACT(doc,"$.geography.Region") |
+--------------------------------------+
| "North America"                      |
+--------------------------------------+
1 row in set (0.00 sec)
```

When the final subpath is a certain value but the other high-level keys are unknown, you can use a wildcard. You can use an asterisk (*) as a wildcard, but note that it will pick up all final keys with the name `Region`:

Example 3-8 *Using a wildcard to find Region data but without having to specify the other keys in the document path*

```
mysql> SELECT JSON_EXTRACT(doc,"$.*.Region") FROM countryinfo WHERE _id='USA';
+-------------------------------+
| JSON_EXTRACT(doc,"$.*.Region") |
+-------------------------------+
| ["North America"]             |
+-------------------------------+
1 row in set (0.00 sec)
```

4

Finding and Getting Data

Simply having data in a MySQL JSON data type column is not much good by itself. Thankfully the engineers at MySQL have provided many extremely useful functions to get into the data, and this chapter delves into the functions for finding and retrieving that data.

All Keys

In Chapter 3, the JSON_KEYS() function was introduced. This function returns the top level of a JSON object as an array. Without the optional path, the function provides the top-level keys. With the optional path, it provides the top-level keys from that particular path.

Format: JSON_KEYS(json_doc[, path])

Example 4-1 *JSON_KEYS with top level of JSON document*

```
mysql> SELECT JSON_KEYS(doc) FROM countryinfo WHERE _id = 'USA';
+---------------------------------------------------------------------------+
| JSON_KEYS(doc)                                                            |
|                                                                           |
+---------------------------------------------------------------------------+
| ["GNP", "_id", "Name", "IndepYear", "geography", "government", "demographics"] |
+---------------------------------------------------------------------------+
1 row in set (0.00 sec)
```

Example 4-2 *JSON_KEYS with optional key to use as top level for reporting*

```
mysql> SELECT JSON_KEYS(doc,"$.geography") FROM countryinfo WHERE _id = 'USA';
+-----------------------------------------+
| JSON_KEYS(doc,"$.geography")            |
+-----------------------------------------+
| ["Region", "Continent", "SurfaceArea"]  |
+-----------------------------------------+
1 row in set (0.00 sec)

mysql>
```

NOTE *Refer to Examples 3-7 and 3-8 in Chapter 3 for specifying deeper-level keys and wildcard characters with a document.*

Searching for a Key

Suppose you have a valid JSON document in a column or row in a table and you need to search for a certain key in that data. Or you need to search for every instance of a certain key in the data (such as a second phone number, additional e-mail addresses, and the like). JSON_CONTAINS_PATH uses the second argument, either ONE or ALL, to determine whether the key will be returned after finding only the first occurrence or finding all of the keys from the path provided as the third (and later) argument. In the next example, there is a match in the specific document to the geography key. JSON_CONTAINS_PATH() returns 1 (true) if the desired key is located in the document. In Example 4-3, the geography key is located, so 1 is returned. A 0 would be returned if the document/columns did not have the desired key.

Format: JSON_CONTAINS_PATH(json_doc, one_or_all, path[, path] ...)

Example 4-3 *JSON_CONTAINS_PATH used to search for key geography*

```
mysql> SELECT JSON_CONTAINS_PATH(doc,"ONE","$.geography") FROM countryinfo WHERE _id='USA';
+-----------------------------------------------+
| JSON_CONTAINS_PATH(doc,"ONE","$.geography")   |
+-----------------------------------------------+
|                                          1    |
+-----------------------------------------------+
1 row in set (0.00 sec)

mysql>
```

Searching for a Path

The various items in a JSON document have keys that are like stepping stones across a stream that let you navigate a path through the document. The key part of the key/value pair is a stepping stone to data. You can also search for multiple keys using a single JSON_CONTAINS_PATH statement. The following example is looking for both the geography and government keys. Both keys must be present for the server to return 1.

Format: JSON_CONTAINS_PATH(json_doc, one_or_all, path[, path] ...)

Example 4-4 *Searching for geography and government keys in the data*

```
mysql> SELECT JSON_CONTAINS_PATH(doc,"ONE","$.geography","$.government") FROM
countryinfo WHERE _id='USA';
+-----------------------------------------------------------------+
| JSON_CONTAINS_PATH(doc,"ONE","$.geography","$.government")       |
+-----------------------------------------------------------------+
|                                                            1    |
+-----------------------------------------------------------------+
1 row in set (0.00 sec)

mysql>
```

The second argument in this function is either ONE or ALL. Use ONE when one key exists at least once in the path; use ALL when you want to find all keys present. In this example, a 0 is returned, which indicates that there is a geography key in the document/column but not a governmentx key. So the server reports no match.

Example 4-5 *Failure using JSON_CONTAINS_PATH, indicated by the 0 because there is no governmentx key within the data*

```
mysql> SELECT JSON_CONTAINS_PATH(doc,"ALL","$.geography","$.governmentx") FROM
countryinfo WHERE _id='USA';
+-------------------------------------------------------------------+
| JSON_CONTAINS_PATH(doc,"ALL","$.geography","$.governmentx") |
+-------------------------------------------------------------------+
|                                                               0 |
+-------------------------------------------------------------------+
1 row in set (0.00 sec)

mysql>
```

Searching for a Value

Use JSON_CONTAINS() to determine whether the value of specified key matches a specified value. This is an equivalency function: Does A equal B? In this example, the IndepYear does match the value 1776 for the document with the _id value equal to USA.

Format: JSON_CONTAINS(json_doc, val[, path])

Example 4-6 *Using JSON_CONTAINS to determine whether the value of IndepYear of this record equals 1776*

```
mysql> SELECT JSON_CONTAINS(doc,"1776","$.IndepYear") FROM countryinfo WHERE _id='USA';
+-----------------------------------------+
| JSON_CONTAINS(doc,"1776","$.IndepYear") |
+-----------------------------------------+
|                                       1 |
+-----------------------------------------+
1 row in set (0.00 sec)

mysql>
```

JSON_SEARCH() returns the position or key of a value. The preceding functions provided the value of given a key.

Example 4-7   *Where is the United States in the path of this data?*

```
mysql> SELECT JSON_SEARCH(doc,"ONE", "United States") FROM countryinfo WHERE _id='usa';
+------------------------------------------+
| JSON_SEARCH(doc,"ONE", "United States") |
+------------------------------------------+
| "$.Name"                                 |
+------------------------------------------+
1 row in set (0.00 sec)

mysql>
```

This function will also check the full path and return matching keys. Note that this is searching on the value to return the key. The preceding examples were looking for the values given a key, while JSON_SEARCH returns keys given values. This function will provide the full path of the key for the given value.

Example 4-8   *Where is North America in this JSON document? JSON_SEARCH provides a way to find the key given a value.*

```
mysql> SELECT JSON_SEARCH(doc,"ONE", "North America") FROM countryinfo WHERE _id='usa';
+------------------------------------------+
| JSON_SEARCH(doc,"ONE", "North America") |
+------------------------------------------+
| "$.geography.Region"                     |
+------------------------------------------+
1 row in set (0.00 sec)

mysql>
```

5

Changing Data

MySQL provides many functions for the creation and modification of data. JSON documents can contain objects, arrays, and combinations thereof that can be confusing at first glance. But these functions are powerful and easy to master.

Using Arrays

The JSON standard proclaims that array values shall be of type string, number, object, Boolean, or null. Arrays are very handy for storing multiple values and, unlike objects, they do not need to be in pairs. Remember that arrays are bound by square brackets, [and], but objects are bound by curly brackets, { and }.

Because it would be messy to adulterate the countryinfo table, a new database schema and table need to be created. Example 5-1 creates a new schema named testjson, creates a table named y, and inserts some sample data.

Format: JSON_ARRAY([val[, val] ...])

Example 5-1   *Creating a new database and table using the JSON data type*

```
mysql> CREATE DATABASE testjson; USE testjson;
Database changed
mysql> CREATE TABLE y (x JSON);
Query OK, 0 rows affected (0.05 sec)

mysql> INSERT INTO y VALUES (JSON_ARRAY('A','B','C'));
Query OK, 1 row affected (0.01 sec)

mysql>
```

This new array has three items: $[0]$ is set to "A", $[1]$ is set to "B", and $[2]$ is set to "C". Those accustomed to programming languages that start counting from 1 need to make a mental note because array elements in JSON documents start with 0.

Example 5-2   *Data from the new table*

```
mysql> SELECT * FROM y;
+-----------------+
| x               |
+-----------------+
| ["A", "B", "C"] |
+-----------------+
1 row in set (0.00 sec)
```

Appending Arrays

Arrays may need to be augmented. You can use JSON_ARRAY_APPEND to append values to the end of the designated arrays within a JSON document and then return the result. It will return a NULL if any argument is NULL.

The server will report an error if the json_doc argument is not a valid JSON document, any path argument is not a valid path expression, or the expression contains a * or ** wildcard. Note that the path/value pairs are evaluated from the left to the right. The document that is produced by evaluating one pair becomes the new value against which the next pair is evaluated; every new evaluation starts fresh on the latest version of the document that is being processed. And remember that the first element in an array is at $[0], the second is at $[1], and so on. It is easy to append a wildcard (*) to $[0], as shown in Example 5-3.

Format: JSON_ARRAY_APPEND(json_doc, path, val[, path, val] ...)

Example 5-3   *Appending the $[0] value*

```
mysql> UPDATE y SET x=JSON_ARRAY_APPEND(x,"$[0]","*");
Query OK, 1 row affected (0.01 sec)
Rows matched: 1  Changed: 1  Warnings: 0

mysql> SELECT * FROM y;
+------------------------+
| x                      |
+------------------------+
| [["A", "*"], "B", "C"] |
+------------------------+
1 row in set (0.00 sec)
```

Now $[0] is set to "A", "*". Another way to think about the change made in Example 5-3 is that $[0] is itself a new array within the previous array.

Note that the data has to exist before it can be appended or it will be postpended.

Example 5-4   *Appending data*

```
mysql> UPDATE y SET x=JSON_ARRAY_APPEND(x,"$","#");
Query OK, 1 row affected (0.01 sec)
Rows matched: 1  Changed: 1  Warnings: 0

mysql> SELECT * FROM y;
+-----------------------------+
| x                           |
+-----------------------------+
| [["A", "*"], "B", "C", "#"] |
+-----------------------------+
1 row in set (0.01 sec)
```

It is also possible to insert multiple values at once. This is more efficient than sending multiple queries, because each query has to have the user authenticated, syntax checked, query plan generated, and then the query is executed. If possible, you'll find that it pays to do as much as possible in "one trip" to the server.

Example 5-5 *Updating data*

```
mysql> UPDATE y SET x=JSON_ARRAY_APPEND(x,"$[1]","@","$[3]","+");
Query OK, 1 row affected (0.00 sec)
Rows matched: 1  Changed: 1  Warnings: 0

mysql> SELECT * FROM y;
+----------------------------------------------+
| x                                            |
+----------------------------------------------+
| [["A", "*"], ["B", "@"], "C", ["#", "+"]]    |
+----------------------------------------------+
1 row in set (0.00 sec)

mysql>
```

Inserting into an Array

JSON_ARRAY_INSERT() is very similar to JSON_ARRAY_APPEND(), but, as the name of the function states, a new value is inserted, instead of appended, at the desired location. It will return a NULL if any argument is NULL. The server will report an error if the json_doc argument is not a valid JSON document, any path argument is not a valid path expression, or the expression contains a * or ** wildcard. Note that the path/value pairs are evaluated from the left to the right. The document that is produced by evaluating one pair becomes the new value against which the next pair is evaluated; every new evaluation starts fresh on the latest version of the document that is being processed.

Format: JSON_ARRAY_INSERT(json_doc, path, val [, path, val] ...)

Example 5-6 *Inserting data*

```
mysql> UPDATE y SET x=JSON_ARRAY_INSERT(x,"$[0]","&");
Query OK, 1 row affected (0.01 sec)
Rows matched: 1  Changed: 1  Warnings: 0
```

```
mysql> SELECT * FROM y;
+-----------------------------------------------------+
| x                                                   |
+-----------------------------------------------------+
| ["&", ["A", "*"], ["B", "@"], "C", ["#", "+"]]      |
+-----------------------------------------------------+
1 row in set (0.00 sec)
mysql>
```

The array changes, with $[0] now set to the new value ("&") and the others values shifted down. In addition, multiple inserts can be done at the same time.

Example 5-7 *Multiple changes simultaneously made by JSON_ARRAY_INSERT*

```
mysql> UPDATE y SET x=JSON_ARRAY_INSERT(x,"$[1]","777","$[3]","999");
Query OK, 1 row affected (0.01 sec)
Rows matched: 1  Changed: 1  Warnings: 0

mysql> SELECT * FROM y;
+-------------------------------------------------------------+
| x                                                           |
+-------------------------------------------------------------+
| ["&", "777", ["A", "*"], "999", ["B", "@"], "C", ["#", "+"]] |
+-------------------------------------------------------------+
1 row in set (0.00 sec)

mysql>
```

Again, in general practice, it is best with relational databases to make multiple changes with one query rather than make many small changes with multiple queries.

Using TRUNCATE Before Adding New Data

For the next few examples, is it best that you "wipe the slate clean" and remove the old data by using the TRUNCATE command and then adding new data. For those unfamiliar with the TRUNCATE command, it removes the data but preserves the underlying table structure.

Example 5-8 *Cleaning the slate of the old array data and starting fresh with an object*

```
mysql> TRUNCATE y;
Query OK, 0 rows affected (0.02 sec)

mysql> INSERT INTO y VALUES('{ "key1" : "value1" }');
Query OK, 1 row affected (0.01 sec)
```

```
mysql> SELECT * FROM y;
+--------------------+
| x                  |
+--------------------+
| {"key1": "value1"} |
+--------------------+
1 row in set (0.00 sec)

mysql>
```

Using JSON_INSERT

You can use JSON_INSERT to insert values into a JSON document. Although it is similar to JSON_SET, JSON_SET is used with keys and values already existing in the document, while JSON_INSERT adds new data. A path/value pair for an already existing path in the document is ignored, and it does not overwrite the existing document value. If a path/value pair does not match a path in the document, it is ignored and has no effect. The server will report an error if the json_doc argument is not a valid JSON document, any path argument is not a valid path expression, or the expression contains a * or ** wildcard. Again note that the path/value pairs are evaluated from the left to the right.

Format: JSON_INSERT(json_doc, path, val[, path, val] ...)

Example 5-9 *Using JSON_INSERT*

```
mysql> UPDATE y SET x = JSON_INSERT(x,'$.key2','value2');
Query OK, 1 row affected (0.01 sec)
Rows matched: 1  Changed: 1  Warnings: 0

mysql> SELECT * FROM y;
+-----------------------------------+
| x                                 |
+-----------------------------------+
| {"key1": "value1", "key2": "value2"} |
+-----------------------------------+
1 row in set (0.00 sec)

mysql>
```

Again, multiple items can be inserted into one statement. The line is read left to right, and after each insert, the next step occurs with the line reexamined including the new element.

Example 5-10   *Multiple inserts with JSON_INSERT*

```
mysql> UPDATE y SET x = JSON_INSERT(x,'$.key1','value1x',"$.key3","value3");
Query OK, 1 row affected (0.01 sec)
Rows matched: 1  Changed: 1  Warnings: 0

mysql> SELECT  * FROM y;
+-------------------------------------------------------------+
| x                                                           |
+-------------------------------------------------------------+
| {"key1": "value1", "key2": "value2", "key3": "value3"}      |
+-------------------------------------------------------------+
1 row in set (0.00 sec)

mysql>
```

Note that in Example 5-10, the query wanted to reset the values for key1 but failed. Why? Because insert is not the same as replace, and JSON_INSERT does *not* replace an existing value. However the $.key3 information was processed by the server. Although half the query worked as desired, there was no warning or error issued on the half that was not performed. If you use this function, you need to be very careful, because this could lead to major problems later. It would be very easy to presume that key1 has the value of *value1x* in this case, when it does not—thus database administrators and developers gather gray hairs. Refer to the next section for a possible alternative.

Using JSON_REPLACE

Use JSON_REPLACE for updating existing values in a JSON document. The path/value pair for an existing path in the document overwrites the existing value in the document with the new value. The path/value pair for a path that is nonexistent in the document is ignored and has no effect. The server will report an error if the json_doc argument is not a valid JSON document, any path argument is not a valid path expression, or the expression contains a * or ** wildcard. The path/value pairs are evaluated from the left to the right.

Format: JSON_REPLACE(json_doc, path, val [, path, val] ...)

Example 5-11   *Using JSON_REPLACE to update values*

```
mysql> SELECT * FROM y;
+-------------------------------------------------------------+
| x                                                           |
+-------------------------------------------------------------+
| {"key1": "value1", "key2": "value2", "key3": "value3"}      |
+-------------------------------------------------------------+
1 row in set (0.00 sec)
```

```
mysql> UPDATE y SET x = JSON_REPLACE(x,"$.key1","Value1A","$.key3","VALUE-3");
Query OK, 1 row affected (0.01 sec)
Rows matched: 1  Changed: 1  Warnings: 0

mysql> SELECT * FROM y;
+--------------------------------------------------------------+
| x                                                            |
+--------------------------------------------------------------+
| {"key1": "Value 1A", "key2": "value2", "key3": "VALUE-3"} |
+--------------------------------------------------------------+
1 row in set (0.00 sec)

mysql>
```

Note that JSON_REPLACE will *not insert* a new value:

Example 5-12 *JSON_REPLACE will not insert a new value; use JSON_INSERT instead.*

```
mysql> UPDATE y SET x = JSON_REPLACE(x,"$.key1","Value1A","$.key3","VALUE-3","$.key4","value4");
Query OK, 0 rows affected (0.00 sec)
Rows matched: 1  Changed: 0  Warnings: 0

mysql> select * from y;
+-----------------------------------------------------------+
| x                                                         |
+-----------------------------------------------------------+
| {"key1": "Value1A", "key2": "value2", "key3": "VALUE-3"} |
+-----------------------------------------------------------+
1 row in set (0.00 sec)
```

JSON_REMOVE

The counterpart to JSON_SET, which is discussed next, is JSON_REMOVE, which is used to delete data from the JSON document. If the element to be removed does not exist in the document, the server does not denote it as an error and it does not affect the document. The server will report an error, however, if the json_doc argument is not a valid JSON document, any path argument is not a valid path expression, or the expression contains a * or ** wildcard. The path/value pairs are evaluated from the left to the right.

Format: JSON_REMOVE(json_doc, path[, path] ...)

Example 5-13 *Using JSON_REMOVE to change a document*

```
mysql> SELECT * FROM y;
+------------------------------------------------------------+
| x                                                          |
+------------------------------------------------------------+
| {"key1": "Value 1A", "key2": "value2", "key3": "VALUE-3"} |
+------------------------------------------------------------+
1 row in set (0.00 sec)
```

```
mysql> UPDATE y SET x = JSON_REMOVE(x,"$.key2");
Query OK, 1 row affected (0.00 sec)
Rows matched: 1  Changed: 1  Warnings: 0

mysql> SELECT * FROM y;
+-------------------------------------------+
| x                                         |
+-------------------------------------------+
| {"key1": "Value 1A", "key3": "VALUE-3"}   |
+-------------------------------------------+
`1 row in set (0.00 sec)

mysql>
```

JSON_REMOVE will remove one or more key/value pairs. When all the key/value pairs need to be removed, it may be easier to use JSON_SET and set the document to a blank or NULL rather than specify each key for the given document.

JSON_SET

The JSON_SET function inserts or updates data in a JSON document and returns the result. If the path/value pair for an existing path is found in the document, the new value will overwrite the old value. But if the path/value pair is nonexistent in the path of the document, it will be added to the document or the member will be added to the object and associated with the new value. If a position value is past the end of an existing array, it will be extended with the new value. The server will report an error if the json_doc argument is not a valid JSON document, any path argument is not a valid path expression, or the expression contains a * or ** wildcard. The path/value pairs are evaluated from the left to the right.

Format: JSON_SET(json_doc, path, val[, path, val] ...)

Example 5-14 *Using JSON_SET to replace the value of "$.key1" and to add a new value for "$.key99"*

```
mysql> SELECT * FROM y;
+-------------------------------------------+
| x                                         |
+-------------------------------------------+
| {"key1": "Value 1A", "key3": "VALUE-3"}   |
+-------------------------------------------+
1 row in set (0.00 sec)
```

```
mysql> UPDATE y SET x = JSON_SET(x,"$.key1","Value 1X","$.key99","Value-99");
Query OK, 1 row affected (0.00 sec)
Rows matched: 1  Changed: 1  Warnings: 0

mysql> SELECT * FROM y;
+----------------------------------------------------------------+
| x                                                              |
+----------------------------------------------------------------+
| {"key1": "Value 1X", "key3": "VALUE-3", "key99": "Value-99"} |
+----------------------------------------------------------------+
1 row in set (0.00 sec)

mysql>
```

JSON_SET will set values for an already defined key (the value of "key1" was changed from "Value 1A" to "Value 1X"). Nonexistent key/values are inserted as directed. Existing keys that are not changed by JSON_SET remain unchanged.

JSON_UNQUOTE

The JSON standards describe how keys and values can be *quoted* to improve their integrity as they are transferred about. Unfortunately, this protection may not be needed by the downstream function or application and should be stripped. Although the function or application can be engineered to do this, it is often much simpler to have the database do this work. And it can be aliased with the ->> operator.

Format: JSON_UNQUOTE(json_val)

Example 5-15 *JSON_UNQUOTE with JSON_EXTRACT, and aliased with the ->> operator*

```
mysql> SELECT * FROM y;
+----------------------------------------------------------------+
| x                                                              |
+----------------------------------------------------------------+
| {"key1": "Value 1X", "key3": "VALUE-3", "key99": "Value-99"} |
+----------------------------------------------------------------+
1 row in set (0.00 sec)

mysql> SELECT JSON_EXTRACT(x,"$.key1") FROM y;
+--------------------------+
| JSON_EXTRACT(x,"$.key1") |
+--------------------------+
| "Value 1X"               |
+--------------------------+
1 row in set (0.00 sec)
```

```
mysql> SELECT JSON_UNQUOTE(JSON_EXTRACT(x,"$.key1")) FROM y;
+-------------------------------------------+
| JSON_UNQUOTE(JSON_EXTRACT(x,"$.key1")) |
+-------------------------------------------+
| Value 1X                                  |
+-------------------------------------------+
1 row in set (0.00 sec)

mysql> SELECT x->>"$.key1" FROM y;
+--------------+
| x->>"$.key1" |
+--------------+
| Value 1X     |
+--------------+
1 row in set (0.00 sec)

mysql>
```

Whether you use the ->> operator instead of JSON_UNQUOTE with JSON_
EXTRACT is a matter of choice, readability, and style. But older versions of
MySQL do not have the ->> operator (MySQL 5.7.13 was its introduction).

The Three JSON_MERGE Functions

There are three JSON_MERGE functions: JSON_MERGE, JSON_MERGE_
PRESERVE, and JSON_MERGE_PATCH. These are very easy to mistake for
one another, but they produce a different effect on the data. To add to any
possible confusion, JSON_MERGE is actually a synonym for JSON_MERGE_
PRESERVE, which means there are two functions with three names—that is,
before JSON_MERGE was deprecated in MySQL version 8.0.3. It will likely be
removed in some future release. JSON_MERGE_PRESERVE was introduced
in MySQL 5.7.22, and you need to be careful in dealing with earlier versions
to avoid confusion and frustration.

So why three separate merge functions? The original JSON_MERGE did
not act like similar functions used in programming languages like Python.
Feedback from early users was mixed, with some loving the original while
others wanted it to match JSON merge functions in their favorite language.

So what does the standard say? Well, not so much in this case. RFC 7159
states that object names should be unique. The implications are that duplicates
are not supposed to happen, and the implementation is left up to the
developer. So JSON_MERGE_PATCH was created to pair with the original
function, now renamed MYSQL_JSON_PRESERVE.

So what are the differences between JSON_MERGE/JSON_MERGE_ PRESERVE and JSON_MERGE_PATCH? JSON_MERGE/JSON_MERGE_ PRESERVE merges two or more JSON documents and returns the merged result. JSON_MERGE_PATCH merges two or more JSON documents, returns the merged result without preserving members having duplicate keys, and drops any member in the first object whose key is matched in the second object.

Example 5-16 clearly shows the JSON_MERGE/JSON_MERGE_PRESERVE cleaning and merging the two JSON objects while preserving all the values but JSON_MERGE_PATCH, keeping only the latest versions of the key/value pairs after the merge.

Example 5-16 *How the various JSON_MERGE functions operate. Be sure to check your version of MySQL to ensure that your query works as desired.*

```
mysql> SELECT JSON_MERGE('{ "odds" : 1, "evens" : 2 }','{ "odds": 3, "evens" : 4 }');
+----------------------------------------------------------------------+
| JSON_MERGE('{ "odds" : 1, "evens" : 2 }','{ "odds": 3, "evens" : 4 }') |
+----------------------------------------------------------------------+
| {"odds": [1, 3], "evens": [2, 4]}                                     |
+----------------------------------------------------------------------+
1 row in set, 1 warning (0.00 sec)

mysql> SELECT JSON_MERGE_PRESERVE('{ "odds" : 1, "evens" : 2 }','{ "odds": 3, "evens" : 4 }');
+------------------------------------------------------------------------------+
| JSON_MERGE_PRESERVE('{ "odds" : 1, "evens" : 2 }','{ "odds": 3, "evens" : 4 }') |
+------------------------------------------------------------------------------+
| {"odds": [1, 3], "evens": [2, 4]}                                             |
+------------------------------------------------------------------------------+
1 row in set (0.00 sec)

mysql> select JSON_MERGE_PATCH('{ "odds" : 1, "evens" : 2 }','{ "odds": 3, "evens" : 4 }');
+----------------------------------------------------------------------------+
| JSON_MERGE_PATCH('{ "odds" : 1, "evens" : 2 }','{ "odds": 3, "evens" : 4 }') |
+----------------------------------------------------------------------------+
| {"odds": 3, "evens": 4}                                                     |
+----------------------------------------------------------------------------+
1 row in set (0.00 sec)
```

JSON_MERGE

The JSON_MERGE function has undergone a lot of changes since the first version came to light. The original intent was fairly simple, as can be seen in Example 5-17.

Format: JSON_MERGE(json_doc, json_doc[, json_doc] ...)

Example 5-17   *Merging two JSON documents (prior to MySQL 5.7.20)*

```
mysql> select JSON_MERGE('{ "odds" : 1, "evens" : 2 }','{ "odds": 3, "evens" : 4 }');
+------------------------------------------------------------------------+
| JSON_MERGE('{ "odds" : 1, "evens" : 2 }','{ "odds": 3, "evens" : 4 }') |
+------------------------------------------------------------------------+
| {"odds": [1, 3], "evens": [2, 4]}                                      |
+------------------------------------------------------------------------+
1 row in set (0.00 sec)
mysql>
```

The two documents had their adjacent keys matched and then their values merged. Depending on the data type, the array or object was combined into one of its data types. A scalar is auto-wrapped as an array and merged as an array. And an adjacent array and object were merged by auto-wrapping the object as an array and merging them as two arrays.

Example 5-18   *Using JSON_MERGE to combine data*

```
mysql> SELECT * from y;
+-----------------------------------------------------------+
| x                                                         |
+-----------------------------------------------------------+
| {"key1": "Value 1X", "key3": "VALUE-3", "key99": "Value-99"} |
+-----------------------------------------------------------+
1 row in set (0.00 sec)

mysql> SELECT JSON_MERGE(x->"$",'{ "key2" : "Buzz" }') FROM y;
+----------------------------------------------------------------------+
| JSON_MERGE(x->"$",'{ "key2" : "Buzz" }')                             |
+----------------------------------------------------------------------+
| {"key1": "Value 1X", "key2": "Buzz", "key3": "VALUE-3", "key99": "Value-99"} |
+----------------------------------------------------------------------+
1 row in set (0.00 sec)

mysql>
```

Notice in Example 5-18 that the keys are sorted!

There was an issue, however, with the "last version wins" order of precedence, which is common in most scripting languages such as PHP's json_merge function. And this approach would be more consistent with other MySQL JSON functions. So JSON_MERGE will change with the latest release of MySQL. Example 5-18 shows two arrays in the SQL statement SELECT JSON_MERGE('{ "odds" : 1, "evens" : 2 }','{ "odds": 3, "evens" : 4 }'); and with last version wins, Example 5-19 shows the output.

Example 5-19 *JSON_MERGE and last version wins precedence (MySQL 8.0.3 and later)*

```
mysql> SELECT JSON_MERGE('{ "odds" : 1, "evens" : 2 }','{ "odds": 3, "evens" : 4 }');
+-----------------------------------------------------------------------+
| JSON_MERGE('{ "odds" : 1, "evens" : 2 }','{ "odds": 3, "evens" : 4 }') |
+-----------------------------------------------------------------------+
| {"odds": [3], "evens": [ 4]}                                          |
+-----------------------------------------------------------------------+
1 row in set (0.00 sec)
```

JSON_MERGE_PRESERVE

The JSON_MERGE_PRESERVE function was created to provide the function-ality of the original JSON_MERGE where last version wins was not consid-ered. Example 5-17 in the preceding section shows how the JSON_MERGE function performs for MySQL 5.7.

Format: JSON_MERGE_PRESERVE(json_doc, json_doc[, json_doc] ...)

JSON_DEPTH

JSON_DEPTH reports the JSON document's maximum depth, or a NULL if there is no document. Empty arrays, objects, and scalars will have a depth of 1. An array containing only elements of depth 1 or a nonempty object containing only member values of depth 1 has a depth of 2. Past that, the depth is greater than 2.

Format: JSON_DEPTH(json_doc)

Example 5-20 *Using JSON_DEPTH*

```
mysql> SELECT JSON_DEPTH(doc), JSON_KEYS(doc) FROM countryinfo WHERE _id = 'USA';
+-----------------+----------------------------------------------------------------------+
| JSON_DEPTH(doc) | JSON_KEYS(doc) |
+-----------------+----------------------------------------------------------------------+
|               3 | ["GNP", "_id", "Name", "IndepYear", "geography", "government", "demographics"] |
+-----------------+----------------------------------------------------------------------+
1 row in set (0.00 sec)
```

JSON_LENGTH

JSON_LENGTH reports the length of a JSON document or the length of a path if one is provided. It is easy to see where the information comes from when used with the JSON_KEYS function.

Format: JSON_LENGTH(json_doc[, path])

Example 5-21   *Using JSON_LENGTH*

```
mysql> SELECT JSON_KEYS(doc), JSON_LENGTH(doc) FROM countryinfo LIMIT 1;
+------------------------------------------------------------------------+------------------+
| JSON_KEYS(doc)                                                         | JSON_LENGTH(doc) |
+------------------------------------------------------------------------+------------------+
| ["GNP", "_id", "Name", "IndepYear", "geography", "government", "demographics"] |                7 |
+------------------------------------------------------------------------+------------------+
1 row in set (0.00 sec)
```

The length of a document is determined as follows: Scalars have a length of 1. Array length is the number of items in the array, and objects are the number of objects in the array. Nested arrays or objects are not counted. In Example 5-22, you can see that the output of JSON_KEYS is the corresponding length of the JSON document.

Example 5-22   *Using JSON_LENGTH to investigate a second-level document path*

```
mysql> SELECT JSON_KEYS(doc,'$.geography'),
           JSON_LENGTH(doc,'$.geography')
           FROM countryinfo LIMIT 1;
+-------------------------------------------+---------------------------------+
| json_keys(doc,'$.geography')              | json_length(doc,'$.geography')  |
+-------------------------------------------+---------------------------------+
| ["Region", "Continent", "SurfaceArea"]    |                               3 |
+-------------------------------------------+---------------------------------+
1 row in set (0.00 sec)
```

JSON_TYPE

The JSON_TYPE function returns a UTF8MB4 string reporting on the contents of a JSON value—array, object, integer, double, and null.

Format: JSON_TYPE(json_val)

Example 5-23   *Using JSON_TYPE to determine the data type*

```
mysql> SELECT JSON_TYPE('[1,2,3]'),
                            JSON_TYPE('{ "x":"y"}'),
                            JSON_TYPE('123'),
                            JSON_TYPE(NULL)\G
*************************** 1. row ***************************
      JSON_TYPE('[1,2,3]'): ARRAY
JSON_TYPE('{ "x" : "y" }'): OBJECT
          JSON_TYPE('123'): INTEGER
          JSON_TYPE(NULL): NULL
1 row in set (0.00 sec)

mysql>
```

JSON_VALID

Use JSON_VALID on a JSON document to test for validity before attempting an insertion into the database; this can save you a great deal of time.

Format: JSON_VALID(val)

Example 5-24 *Using JSON_VALID to ensure validity of JSON documents*

```
mysql> SELECT JSON_VALID('{ "A" : 1}'),
            JSON_VALID('A'),
            JSON_VALID('"A"')\G
*********************** 1. row **************************
JSON_VALID('{ "A" : 1}'): 1
       JSON_VALID('A'): 0
     JSON_VALID('"A"'): 1
1 row in set (0.00 sec)

mysql>
```

Remember that the MySQL server will reject invalid JSON documents. In Example 5-24 all the expressions are not valid JSON, so the server returns a 0. The first test is a valid JSON object and the third is a valid JSON document. But the second test fails because it is an invalid JSON document.

JSON_STORAGE_SIZE

The JSON_STORAGE_SIZE function reports the size in bytes needed to store the binary representation of the JSON document when it was inserted. This function was introduced in MySQL 5.7.22 and is not found in earlier versions.

Format: JSON_STORAGE_SIZE(json_val)

Example 5-25 *Determining document storage size with JSON_STORAGE_SIZE. The size of a document on disk is roughly 1 gigabyte, but it can be larger while being manipulated in memory.*

```
mysql> SELECT JSON_EXTRACT(doc,'$.Name'),
            JSON_STORAGE_SIZE(doc)
            FROM countryinfo
            WHERE _id IN ("USA","BRA");
+----------------------------+------------------------+
| JSON_EXTRACT(doc,'$.Name') | JSON_STORAGE_SIZE(doc) |
+----------------------------+------------------------+
| "Brazil"                   |                    342 |
| "United States"            |                    338 |
+----------------------------+------------------------+
2 rows in set (0.01 sec)
```

JSON_STORAGE_FREE

The JSON_STORAGE_FREE function reports the amount of storage space that was freed in bytes in its binary representation after it was updated. The updates need to be in place (not a rewrite of the entire document) using JSON_SET, JSON_REMOVE, or JSON_REPLACE. It will return a 0 if the argument is a JSON document in a string.

Format: JSON_STORAGE_FREE(json_val)

Example 5-26 *Using JSON_STORAGE_FREE by changing "This is a string", which is 16 characters, to "a", which is 1 character, or a net change of 15 bytes*

```
mysql> CREATE DATABASE  IF NOT EXISTS test; USE test;
mysql>CREATE TABLE x (id INT UNSIGNED, doc JSON);
mysql>INSERT INTO x VALUES (1,'{"a" : "1"}');
mysql> UPDATE x SET doc = JSON_SET(doc,'$[0]','{ "a" : "This is a string" }');
Query OK, 1 row affected (0.01 sec)
Rows matched: 1  Changed: 1  Warnings: 0

mysql> UPDATE x SET doc = JSON_SET(doc,'$[0]','{ "a" : "a" }');
Query OK, 1 row affected (0.01 sec)
Rows matched: 1  Changed: 1  Warnings: 0

mysql> SELECT JSON_STORAGE_FREE(doc) FROM x;
+------------------------+
| JSON_STORAGE_FREE(doc) |
+------------------------+
|                     15 |
+------------------------+
1 row in set (0.00 sec)
```

6

JSON and
Non-JSON Output

The advantages of traditional relational data and schemaless data are both large. But in some cases, data in a schema needs to be schemaless, or schemaless data needs to be in a schema. Making such changes is easy to do.

JSON-Formatted Data

The various JSON functions supplied by MySQL can also be used to create JSON-formatted output from non-JSON data. Example 6-1 shows non-JSON data output in a non-JSON format, which has been the standard for MySQL for much of its existence.

Example 6-1 *Non-JSON data and output from a relational table*

```
mysql> SELECT city.Name,
              country.Name
         FROM city
         JOIN country ON (city.CountryCode=country.Code)
         LIMIT 5;
+----------------+-------------+
| Name           | Name        |
+----------------+-------------+
| Kabul          | Afghanistan |
| Qandahar       | Afghanistan |
| Herat          | Afghanistan |
| Mazar-e-Sharif | Afghanistan |
| Amsterdam      | Netherlands |
+----------------+-------------+
5 rows in set (0.00 sec)
```

This is a fairly typical example of MySQL output for a regular query— good-old MySQL at its finest. But it's not very useful if that data is needed by something that consumes data in a JSON format.

JSON_OBJECT

The query from Example 6-1 can quickly be adapted to output non-JSON data in a JSON format. JSON objects can easily be created with JSON_OBJECT, but remember that JSON objects contain pairs (key/value pairs), so there cannot be an odd number of arguments.

In Example 6-2, strings are added to the preceding query to create keys for the values. Neither "City" nor "Country" are table row names; both rows are named Name, which can be confusing for casual readers and for the server.

Format: JSON_OBJECT([key, val[, key, val] ...])

Example 6-2   *Using JSON_OBJECT with non-JSON data*

```
mysql> SELECT
    JSON_OBJECT("City", city.Name, "Country", country.Name)
            FROM city
            JOIN country ON (city.CountryCode=country.Code)
            LIMIT 5;
+-------------------------------------------------------------+
| JSON_OBJECT("City", city.Name, "Country", country.Name) |
+-------------------------------------------------------------+
| {"City": "Kabul", "Country": "Afghanistan"}             |
| {"City": "Qandahar", "Country": "Afghanistan"}          |
| {"City": "Herat", "Country": "Afghanistan"}             |
| {"City": "Mazar-e-Sharif", "Country": "Afghanistan"}    |
| {"City": "Amsterdam", "Country": "Netherlands"}         |
+-------------------------------------------------------------+
5 rows in set (0.00 sec)
```

Now the non-JSON data is in a JSON format. You can use both non-JSON and JSON columns as arguments to this function.

JSON_ARRAY

In a similar fashion to using JSON_OBJECT, you can use JSON_ARRAY to create arrays from non-JSON data.

Format: JSON_ARRAY([val[, val] ...])

Example 6-3   *Using JSON_ARRAY with non-JSON data*

```
mysql> SELECT JSON_ARRAY(Code, Name, Capital) FROM country LIMIT 1;
+----------------------------------+
| json_array(Code, Name, Capital) |
+----------------------------------+
| ["ABW", "Aruba", 129]           |
+----------------------------------+
1 row in set (0.00 sec)

mysql>
```

Examples 6-2 and 6-3 show how traditional MySQL data can be formatted as JSON objects or arrays. And, of course, you can mix and match JSON and non-JSON columns into arrays or objects.

Casting

MySQL enables you to cast one data type as another. This includes JSON. Casting from within MySQL has been around for decades before the JSON data type.

Example 6-4 *Casting data as JSON*

```
mysql> SELECT JSON_TYPE(CAST('[1,2]' AS JSON));
+----------------------------------+
| JSON_TYPE(CAST('[1,2]' AS JSON)) |
+----------------------------------+
| ARRAY                            |
+----------------------------------+
1 row in set (0.00 sec)

mysql> SELECT JSON_TYPE(CAST('1' AS JSON));
+----------------------------+
| JSON_TYPE(CAST('1' AS JSON)) |
+----------------------------+
| INTEGER                    |
+----------------------------+
1 row in set (0.00 sec)

mysql>
```

Conversely, JSON data can be cast as other data types:

Example 6-5 *Casting a JSON DOUBLE as unsigned*

```
mysql> SELECT
        CAST(JSON_EXTRACT(doc,"$.demographics.LifeExpectancy") AS unsigned)
            FROM countryinfo
            WHERE _id = 'USA';
+---------------------------------------------------------------------+
| CAST(JSON_EXTRACT(doc,"$.demographics.LifeExpectancy") AS unsigned) |
+---------------------------------------------------------------------+
|                                                                  77 |
+---------------------------------------------------------------------+
1 row in set (0.00 sec)
```

Make sure that you provide the full path of the JSON key you are searching, or the server will return NULL. It would also be wise to choose a style and stick with it. Example 6-5 is much easier to read than

```
SELECT CAST(doc->>"$.demographics.LifeExpectancy" AS unsigned) FROM countryinfo
WHERE _id = 'USA';
```

using the shortcuts for JSON_UNQUOTE wrapped around JSON_EXTRACT, but older versions of MySQL will not be able to handle that query. Wildcards will also cause problems, as shown in Example 6-6.

Example 6-6   *How wildcards can affect casting*

```
mysql> SELECT json_extract(doc,"$.demographics.LifeExpectancy")
          FROM countryinfo
          WHERE _id = 'USA';
+------------------------------------------------------+
| json_extract(doc,"$.demographics.LifeExpectancy")    |
+------------------------------------------------------+
| 77.0999984741211                                     |
+------------------------------------------------------+
1 row in set (0.00 sec)

mysql> SELECT CAST(doc->>"$.demographics.LifeExpectancy" AS unsigned) FROM countryinfo WHERE _id = 'USA';
+--------------------------------------------------------+
| CAST(doc->>"$.demographics.LifeExpectancy" AS unsigned) |
+--------------------------------------------------------+
|                                                     77 |
+--------------------------------------------------------+
1 row in set, 1 warning (0.00 sec)

mysql> SELECT CAST(doc->>"$.*.LifeExpectancy" AS unsigned) FROM countryinfo WHERE _id = 'USA';
+----------------------------------------------+
| CAST(doc->>"$.*.LifeExpectancy" AS unsigned) |
+----------------------------------------------+
|                                            0 |
+----------------------------------------------+
1 row in set, 1 warning (0.00 sec)

mysql> show warnings;
+---------+------+-------------------------------------------------------------+
| Level   | Code | Message                                                     |
+---------+------+-------------------------------------------------------------+
| Warning | 1292 | Truncated incorrect INTEGER value: '[77.0999984741211]'     |
+---------+------+-------------------------------------------------------------+
1 row in set (0.00 sec)

mysql>
```

Example 6-6 illustrates how using a wildcard in the path in JSON_ EXTRACT will return an array, while without the data, it is a double. In the first query, where the path $.demographics.LifeExpectancy is fully provided, it generates a warning: "Truncated incorrect INTEGER value: '[77.0999984741211]'" (use SHOW WARNINGS; to display the warnings). This can usually be ignored. But when the path includes a wildcard, such as $.*.LifeExpectancy, the server cannot cast the value returned to unsigned, because it is an array (note the square brackets around the INTEGER value). It may be intuitive to some that the two queries in Example 6-6 are pretty much equivalent, but they are not seen that way by the server.

When in doubt, cast your values to what you need. This is especially important when you're matching data values with indexes, because it provides the query optimizer with valuable information for building query plans.

Non-JSON Output

Transforming JSON data into temporary relational tables is done with the JSON_TABLE function, which, as of this writing, is available only as a Developer Milestone Release of MySQL 8.0.3, from http://labs.mysql.com; hopefully, it will become part of the generally available release of MySQL 8.

The power to map JSON data into temporary relational tables and then query from those tables opens up the power of relational data processing without having to establish generated columns, using hard-to-debug stored procedures, or creating views. Once we have the relational table, it is easy to use like any other relational table, and we can winnow down the results with the WHERE clause. In Example 6-7, two JSON key/value pairs are extracted, formatted, and then returned in a table.

Format: JSON_TABLE(doc, path, columns (name type PATH path),...) AS Temptable-name

Example 6-7   *Using JSON_TABLE to convert JSON data into a relational table*

```
mysql> SELECT country_name, IndyYear
    FROM countryinfo,
    JSON_TABLE(doc, "$" COLUMNS (
      country_name CHAR(20) PATH "$.Name",
      IndyYear INT PATH "$.IndepYear")) as stuff
    WHERE IndyYear > 1992;
+----------------+----------+
| country_name   | IndyYear |
+----------------+----------+
| Czech Republic | 1993     |
| Eritrea        | 1993     |
| Palau          | 1994     |
| Slovakia       | 1993     |
+----------------+----------+
4 rows in set, 67 warnings (0.08 sec)

mysql>
```

Note that the two columns—country_name and IndyYear—are named only within the JSON_TABLE. The first argument to the function is the JSON column in the table to be used and then the path is specified. The $ path can be used to specify the entire document, or a subpath can be specified.

This query also generated 67 warnings! Twenty of those can be easily removed by upping the CHAR(20) field for country_name to something longer, such as CHAR(50). Truncating data can be dangerous, and it would take some work to check all the documents to find the longest Name and then adjust the query to match. The other 47 warnings are invalid castings of a

NULL to an integer. For this particular query, the desired result was for countries with years of independence since 1993; it does not matter. But it would matter if the desired result was, for example, independence years before 1515 as they would not collect the records with NULL in the IndyYear column.

Missing Data

An interesting feature of JSON_TABLE is that it offers you the ability to specify what to do when data is missing. Unlike a relational column, where missing or NULL values can be stored, the JSON document has no guarantee that all desired key/value pairs exist.

Example 6-8 *Sample data for JSON_TABLE*

```
mysql> SELECT * FROM t1;
+-----+--------------------------+
| _id | doc                      |
+-----+--------------------------+
|   1 | {"x": 0, "name": "Bill"} |
|   2 | {"x": 1, "name": "Mary"} |
|   3 | {"name": "Pete"}         |
+-----+--------------------------+
3 rows in set (0.00 sec)

mysql>
```

Example 6-8 has a small dataset, where all the columns have a name key/value pair and the third record is missing an x key/value pair. The DEFAULT ON EMPTY qualifier can be used to provide data for the missing x key/value pair. Example 6-9 shows how to deal with a missing value.

Example 6-9 *JSON_TABLE used with a DEFAULT value for missing data and EXISTS to determine whether the data is available*

```
mysql> SELECT * FROM t1,
       JSON_TABLE(doc,"$" COLUMNS (
       xHasValue INT PATH "$.x" DEFAULT '999' ON EMPTY,
       hasname CHAR(10) EXISTS PATH "$.name",
       mojo CHAR(5) EXISTS PATH "$.mojo"))
       AS t2;
+-----+--------------------------+-----------+---------+------+
| _id | doc                      | xHasValue | hasname | mojo |
+-----+--------------------------+-----------+---------+------+
|   1 | {"x": 0, "name": "Bill"} |         0 | 1       | 0    |
|   2 | {"x": 1, "name": "Mary"} |         1 | 1       | 0    |
|   3 | {"name": "Pete"}         |       999 | 1       | 0    |
+-----+--------------------------+-----------+---------+------+
3 rows in set (0.00 sec)

mysql>
```

When we specify DEFAULT '999' ON EMPTY, the server will return the default value when the desired key/value pair is missing. The third record is missing a value for x, and the value 999 is inserted into the table.

The EXISTS keyword returns a Boolean answer if the referenced key/value pair exists. Because all the records have a name key/value pair, the hasname column shows a 1. But not one of the records has a mojo key/value pair, so a 0 is returned in that column. Example 6-10 shows how to use the Boolean data from JSON_TABLE in a SQL query.

Example 6-10 *Using the Boolean data from JSON_TABLE's EXIST keyword as part of a query*

```
mysql> SELECT * FROM t1,
       JSON_TABLE(doc,"$" COLUMNS (
       xHasValue INT PATH "$.x" DEFAULT '999' ON EMPTY,
       hasname CHAR(10) EXISTS PATH "$.name",
       mojo CHAR(5) EXISTS PATH "$.mojo"))
       AS t2
       WHERE hasname = 1 and xHasValue = 1;
+-----+------------------------------+-----------+---------+------+
| _id | doc                          | xHasValue | hasname | mojo |
+-----+------------------------------+-----------+---------+------+
|   2 | {"x": 1, "name": "Mary"}     |         1 | 1       | 0    |
+-----+------------------------------+-----------+---------+------+
1 row in set (0.01 sec)
```

In this example, the desired data has the hasname column equal to 1 and the xHasValue column equal to 1. By using such queries, you can easily determine whether documents do indeed have certain key/value pairs.

Nested Data

JSON_TABLE also has the ability to walk down the JSON document path and retrieve nested data. In Example 6-11, there are several values of z for each record's y key. The ability to extract each individual value comes from the NESTED PATH option.

Example 6-11 *This name has nested values of key z within the key y.*

```
mysql> SELECT * FROM t2;
+-----+--------------------------------------------------+
| _id | doc                                              |
+-----+--------------------------------------------------+
|  10 | {"x": 1, "y": [{"z": 1}, {"z": 3}]}              |
|  20 | {"x": 2, "y": [{"z": 2}, {"z": 4}]}              |
|  30 | {"x": 33, "y": [{"z": 2}, {"z": 3}, {"z": 4}]}   |
+-----+--------------------------------------------------+
3 rows in set (0.02 sec)

mysql>
```

Extracting all values of z from the y can be done with string-handling functions or some very nasty regular expression code. However, JSON_ TABLE allows walking down paths with nested values. And JSON_TABLE can also provide an ordinal number for returned data.

Example 6-12   *Using the NESTED PATH option with JSON_TABLE to extract all values of z from the y key/value pair*

```
mysql> SELECT * FROM t2,
       JSON_TABLE(doc, "$" COLUMNS (
         myX INT PATH "$.x",
             NESTED PATH "$.y[*]" COLUMNS (
                      myID FOR ORDINALITY,
                      myZ CHAR(10) PATH "$.z")))
            AS tt;
+-----+-------------------------------------------------+------+------+------+
| _id | doc                                             | myX  | myID | myZ  |
+-----+-------------------------------------------------+------+------+------+
|  10 | {"x": 1, "y": [{"z": 1}, {"z": 3}]}             |    1 |    1 | 1    |
|  10 | {"x": 1, "y": [{"z": 1}, {"z": 3}]}             |    1 |    2 | 3    |
|  20 | {"x": 2, "y": [{"z": 2}, {"z": 4}]}             |    2 |    1 | 2    |
|  20 | {"x": 2, "y": [{"z": 2}, {"z": 4}]}             |    2 |    2 | 4    |
|  30 | {"x": 33, "y": [{"z": 2}, {"z": 3}, {"z": 4}]}  |   33 |    1 | 2    |
|  30 | {"x": 33, "y": [{"z": 2}, {"z": 3}, {"z": 4}]}  |   33 |    2 | 3    |
|  30 | {"x": 33, "y": [{"z": 2}, {"z": 3}, {"z": 4}]}  |   33 |    3 | 4    |
+-----+-------------------------------------------------+------+------+------+
7 rows in set (0.00 sec)

mysql>
```

This may seem more confusing than it really is. It can often be helpful to read the SQL statements aloud to aid in comprehension. In Example 6-12, the NESTED PATH of $.y[*] (which also could have been $.y) is searched for any values of z in that path. Or, y becomes its own document and the server searched within it for any values of z.

The FOR ORDINALITY operator allows a running total for each of the values that is broken out in the NESTED PATH operation. The document with the _id of 10 has two ordinal values because there were two z values in that document's y key/value pair. And the document with the _id of 30 has three because its document has three values for z under the y key/value pair.

7

Generated Columns

The MySQL server cannot index JSON columns. Generally, you want indexes to be as small as practicable for speed, and trying to use up to a gigabyte of unstructured data would not be efficient. This situation is similar to that of other data BLOBs. Data from the JSON column, however, can be extracted into a generated column, and that column can be indexed.

There are two types of generated columns. The *virtual* generated column is evaluated when the column is read but before any existing triggers are fired for that column. The *stored* generated column is evaluated and stored when data is either inserted or updated. The default is virtual generated, but both types can be used together in a table.

Virtual generated columns cannot contain subqueries, parameters, variables, stored functions, or user-defined functions. You cannot use the AUTO_INCREMENT attribute in a virtual generated column or base a virtual generated column on a column that uses AUTO_INCREMENT. Foreign-key constraints on a stored generated column cannot use ON UPDATE CASCADE, ON DELETE SET NULL, ON UPDATE SET NULL, ON DELETE SET DEFAULT, or ON UPDATE SET DEFAULT. Also, foreign-key constraints cannot reference a virtual generated column. Several other constraints are detailed in the MySQL user manual that are worth reading at a later time but do not fit in this book.

Using Generated Columns

The keyword AS denotes a generated column. Example 7-1 calculates the taxable amount of an item given the item price and multiplies it by the tax rate. The taxRate is the percentage of the itemPrice to be taxed. The server calculates the taxAmount.

Example 7-1 *Using generated columns to calculate values*

```
mysql> CREATE TABLE taxCalc (itemPrice DECIMAL(10,3),
                 taxRate DECIMAL(10,3),
                 taxAmount DECIMAL(10,3) AS (itemPrice * taxRate));
Query OK, 0 rows affected (0.01 sec)

mysql> INSERT INTO taxCalc (itemPrice, taxRate) VALUES (10.0,0.08), (100.0,0.25);
Query OK, 2 rows affected (0.01 sec)
Records: 2  Duplicates: 0  Warnings: 0

mysql> SELECT * FROM taxCalc;
+-----------+---------+-----------+
| itemPrice | taxRate | taxAmount |
+-----------+---------+-----------+
|    10.000 |   0.080 |     0.800 |
|   100.000 |   0.250 |    25.000 |
+-----------+---------+-----------+
2 rows in set (0.00 sec)

mysql>
```

Note that only the itemPrice and taxRate are entered into the table and the server calculates the taxAmount column.

Columns Generated from JSON

The world_x countryinfo table has a generated column and is a prime example of the MySQL document store table format. The InnoDB storage engine requires a PRIMARY KEY and will pick one, often a poor one, if it's not specified. MySQL will create a column named _id when a collection is created and denote it as the primary key. If there is no _id data in the JSON document column named doc, the column will hold a NULL.

Example 7-2   *How the MySQL document store creates collections*

```
mysql> DESC countryinfo;
+--------+-------------+------+-----+---------+-------------------+
| Field  | Type        | Null | Key | Default | Extra             |
+--------+-------------+------+-----+---------+-------------------+
| doc    | json        | YES  |     | NULL    |                   |
| _id    | varchar(32) | NO   | PRI | NULL    | STORED GENERATED  |
+--------+-------------+------+-----+---------+-------------------+
2 rows in set (0.00 sec)

mysql>
```

A simple DESCRIBE table will show the layout of the table and that there is a stored generated column, but it won't show the actual code for the generation. More details on the Document Store's table are available from SHOW CREATE TABLE than from the DESCRIBE table.

Example 7-3   *In this case, the workings of the GENERATED column are shown.*

```
mysql> SHOW CREATE TABLE countryinfo;
+-------------+-------------------------------------------------------------+
| Table       | Create Table |
+-------------+-------------------------------------------------------------+
| countryinfo | CREATE TABLE 'countryinfo' (
  'doc' json DEFAULT NULL,
  '_id' varchar(32) GENERATED ALWAYS AS (json_unquote(json_extract('doc',_utf8'$._id'))) STORED NOT NULL,
  PRIMARY KEY ('_id')
) ENGINE=InnoDB DEFAULT CHARSET=utf8 |
+-------------+-------------------------------------------------------------+
1 row in set (0.00 sec)
```

A SHOW CREATE TABLE provides the details on the generation of the created table. It is easy to see that the _id column is created from JSON column doc's key/value pair of _id. Note the UTF8 casting of this field.

Any other JSON key (or keys in combination; consult the MySQL manual regarding composite indexes) can be used in a generated column. If you are regularly extracting one key/value pair, it may be faster to use a generated column and index than a generated column to search via SQL.

Example 7-4 *Using ALTER TABLE to add a generated column for PopulationCountry*

```
mysql> ALTER TABLE countryinfo
    -> ADD COLUMN PopulationCountry INT AS
    -> (JSON_UNQUOTE(doc->"$.demographics.Population"));
Query OK, 0 rows affected (0.25 sec)
Records: 0  Duplicates: 0  Warnings: 0
```

It is better to use the STORED GENERATED column option for building indexes. The VIRTUAL GENERATED type is not stored and must be computed at access time, which is a lot of work. With a STORED GENERATED column, the value is materialized in a column that is stored when the data is written. If the structure of the countryinfo table is examined after Example 7-3, you can see that the new column is virtual generated and not stored generated.

Example 7-5 *The description of countryinfo shows the PopulationCountry column setup from Example 7-4, which is a VIRTUAL GENERATED column, which is not desired.*

```
mysql> DESC countryinfo;
+-------------------+-------------+------+-----+---------+-------------------+
| Field             | Type        | Null | Key | Default | Extra             |
+-------------------+-------------+------+-----+---------+-------------------+
| doc               | json        | YES  |     | NULL    |                   |
| _id               | varchar(32) | NO   | PRI | NULL    | STORED GENERATED  |
| PopulationCountry | int(11)     | YES  |     | NULL    | VIRTUAL GENERATED |
+-------------------+-------------+------+-----+---------+-------------------+
3 rows in set (0.06 sec)

mysql>
```

Luckily, it is easy to remove the new columns using ALTER TABLE countryinfo DROP COLUMN PopulationCountry and then reissue the command to create the generated column, but this time with the keyword STORED appended. Checking the description shows that the new PopulationCountry column is indeed a STORED GENERATED column.

Example 7-6 *The description of countryinfo now shows the desired STORED GENERATED PopulationCountry column.*

```
mysql> ALTER TABLE countryinfo ADD COLUMN
  PopulationCountry INT AS
 (doc->>"$.demographics.Population") STORED;
Query OK, 239 rows affected (0.17 sec)
Records: 239  Duplicates: 0  Warnings: 0

mysql> desc countryinfo;
+-------------------+-------------+------+-----+---------+------------------+
| Field             | Type        | Null | Key | Default | Extra            |
+-------------------+-------------+------+-----+---------+------------------+
| doc               | json        | YES  |     | NULL    |                  |
| _id               | varchar(32) | NO   | PRI | NULL    | STORED GENERATED |
| PopulationCountry | int(11)     | YES  |     | NULL    | STORED GENERATED |
+-------------------+-------------+------+-----+---------+------------------+
3 rows in set (0.00 sec)

mysql>
```

One more step is needed to have a SQL usable index on the new column, which will be something along the lines of CREATE INDEX Population_ Index on countryinfo (PopulationCountry); following an index naming convention of your choosing.

Generated Columns: Common Errors

When adding a generated column, the type definition is important. Undersizing the length for a type can lead to some issues.

Example 7-7 *The VARCHAR(20) column was too small for the data when trying to set up a STORED column. The VIRTUAL column, however, was able to be created.*

```
mysql> ALTER TABLE countryinfo ADD COLUMN GovernmentForm VARCHAR(20) GENERATED
ALWAYS AS (doc->>"$.government.GovernmentForm") STORED;
ERROR 1406 (22001): Data too long for column 'GovernmentForm' at row 1
mysql> ALTER TABLE countryinfo ADD COLUMN GovernmentForm VARCHAR(20) GENERATED
ALWAYS AS (doc->>"$.government.GovernmentForm") VIRTUAL;
Query OK, 0 rows affected (0.06 sec)
Records: 0  Duplicates: 0  Warnings: 0
```

The data will need to be studied to see if the virtual generated column has enough useful data after truncation to be useful. It would be useful to examine the raw data to determine exactly how wide the column needs to be to fit all of it in. But on the other hand, only the first several characters may be of interest.

Example 7-8 *Examining the data for the generated column to make sure it is of adequate length. And for this record, it is.*

```
mysql> SELECT * FROM countryinfo WHERE _id = "USA"\G
*************************** 1. row ***************************
            doc: {"GNP": 8510700, "_id": "USA", "Name": "United States", "IndepYear":
1776, "geography": {"Region": "North America", "Continent": "North America", "SurfaceArea":
9363520}, "government": {"HeadOfState": "George W. Bush", "GovernmentForm": "Federal
Republic"}, "demographics": {"Population": 278357000, "LifeExpectancy": 77.0999984741211}}
            _id: USA
PopulationCountry: 278357000
   GovernmentForm: Federal Republic
1 row in set (0.00 sec)
```

The next step would be to use CREATE INDEX. But there is another problem—or an old problem has returned.

Example 7-9 *Attempting to create an index on the virtual generated column returns us to the data that's too long for the column issue.*

```
mysql> ALTER TABLE countryinfo ADD INDEX govrmtform_
idx(GovernmentForm);
ERROR 1406 (22001): Data too long for column 'GovernmentForm' at row 1
```

MySQL 5.7 introduced the WITH VALIDATION clause to ALTER TABLE. It is used to make sure the calculated data is not out of range for the desired column. Using this, combined with trimming the data down to the desired width, provides a way to generate the column into something that can be indexed.

Example 7-10 *Using WITH VALIDATION in the ALTER TABLE statement provides a way to create an easy-to-index column.*

```
mysql> ALTER TABLE countryinfo ADD COLUMN GovernmentForm VARCHAR(20) GENERATED
ALWAYS AS (LEFT(doc->>"$.government.GovernmentForm",20)) VIRTUAL, WITH VALIDATION;
Query OK, 239 rows affected (0.20 sec)
Records: 239  Duplicates: 0  Warnings: 0

mysql> ALTER TABLE countryinfo ADD index govform_idx(GovernmentForm);
Query OK, 0 rows affected (0.10 sec)
Records: 0  Duplicates: 0  Warnings: 0

mysql>
```

8

GeoJSON

MySQL 5.7 offered several new features in addition to the JSON data type, including a vast improvement in geographic information system (GIS) support. MySQL follows the Open Geospatial Consortium (OGC) *OpenGIS Implementation Specification for Geographic information - Simple feature access - Part 2: SQL option*, which proposes extending the SQL RDBMS to support spatial data. MySQL also features functions for converting between spatial values and JSON and follows the GeoJSON specification (RFC 7946) located at http://geojson.org. GeoJSON supports the same geometric and geographic data types as MySQL.

ST_GeomFromGeoJSON

The ST_GeomFromGeoJSON function processes as a GeoJSON-formatted string and returns a geometry. A second optional argument regarding how to handle GeoJSON documents contains geometries with coordinate dimensions higher than a 2; this option can have the value of 1 (default), reject the JSON formatted document and produce an error message; and 2, 3, or 4, accept the document and strip off the coordinates for higher coordinate dimensions. And there is a third and final argument: the Spatial Reference System Identifier (SRID) argument, if given, must be a 32-bit unsigned integer. If not given, the geometry return value has an SRID of 4326. Table 8-1 lists GeoJSON options that are bitmasks, and also lists the permitted values. They can be combined so that a value of 7 is made up of 1, 2, and 4 from the table. The bitmasks for the GeoJSON function are combined to provide more detail or change the style of output.

Example 8-1   *Using ST_GeomFromGeoJSON*

```
mysql> SELECT ST_AsText(ST_GeomFromGeoJSON('{ "type" : "Point", "coordinates" : [99.1, 1.1]}'));
+----------------------------------------------------------------------------------+
| ST_AsText(ST_GeomFromGeoJSON('{ "type" : "Point", "coordinates" : [99.1, 1.1]}')) |
+----------------------------------------------------------------------------------+
| POINT(1.1 99.1)                                                                  |
+----------------------------------------------------------------------------------+
1 row in set (0.01 sec)

mysql>
```

The ST_AsGeomFromGeoJSON function takes a JSON-formatted string and turns it into a geometry. Note that you can wrap this function with

Flag Value	Meaning
0	No options. This is the default.
1	A bounding box is added to the output.
2	A short-format Coordinate Reference System (CRS) Uniform Resource Name (URN) is added to the output. The default format is the short format (EPSG:*srid*).
4	A long-format CRS URN (urn:ogc:def:crs:EPSG::*srid*) is added to the output. This flag overrides flag 2. Option values of 5 and 7 mean the same (a bounding box and a long-format CRS URN).

Table 8-1   *Options for GeoJSON*

ST_AsText to format the output to something more readable. The following, without the ST_AsText, displays the function's usefulness.

Example 8-2 *Not exactly what we wanted from ST_GeomFromGeoJSON*

```
mysql> SELECT  ST_GeomFromGeoJSON('{ "type" : "Point", "coordinates" : [99.1, 1.1]}',4);
+------------------------------------------------------------------------+
| ST_GeomFromGeoJSON('{ "type" : "Point", "coordinates" : [99.1, 1.1]}',4) |
+------------------------------------------------------------------------+
| ◆     fffff◆x@◆◆◆◆◆◆◆?                                                  |
+------------------------------------------------------------------------+
1 row in set (0.00 sec)

mysql>
```

ST_AsGeoJSON

The ST_AsGeoJSON function is the opposite of ST_GeomFromGeoJSON in that takes a geometry and produces a GeoJSON object. Its first option is the number of decimal digits for coordinates, and options can be added, as shown in Example 8-3, to modify the output.

Example 8-3 *Using ST_GeomFromText*

```
mysql> SELECT ST_AsGeoJSON(ST_GeomFromText('POINT(12.3456 23.4567)'),2);
+--------------------------------------------------------------+
| ST_AsGeoJSON(ST_GeomFromText('POINT(12.3456 23.4567)'),2)     |
+--------------------------------------------------------------+
| {"type": "Point", "coordinates": [12.35, 23.46]}              |
+--------------------------------------------------------------+
1 row in set (0.00 sec)
```

The ST_GeomFromText options are bitmasks, which means they can be combined. Table 8-2 shows the values of the bitmask options. With no option specified, the output is shown in Example 8-3.

Option Value	Meaning
1	Reject the document and produce an error. This is the default.
2, 3, 4	Accept the document, stripping off the coordinates at higher coordinate dimensions.

Table 8-2 *Options for ST_GeomFromText*

Example 8-4   *ST_GeomFromText without options*

```
mysql> SELECT ST_AsGeoJSON(ST_GeomFromText('POINT(12.3456 23.4567)'),2,1);
+----------------------------------------------------------------------------+
| ST_AsGeoJSON(ST_GeomFromText('POINT(12.3456 23.4567)'),2,1)                |
+----------------------------------------------------------------------------+
| {"bbox": [12.35, 23.46, 12.35, 23.46], "type": "Point", "coordinates": [12.35, 23.46]}|
+----------------------------------------------------------------------------+
1 row in set (0.00 sec)
```

Option 1 adds a bounding box (bbox), as you can see in Example 8-4. Option 2 adds a short-format CRS URN to the output with the default format being a short format (EPSG:srid). Option 4 adds a long-format CRS URN (urn:ogc:def:crs:EPSG::srid) and overrides option 2. Since the option field is a bitmask, the various options can be combined. Option 3, for example, is option 1 plus option 2.

Example 8-5   *Other options for the ST_GeoJSON function*

```
mysql> SELECT ST_AsGeoJSON(ST_GeomFromText('POINT(12.3456 23.4567)'),2,4);
+------------------------------------------------------------+
| ST_AsGeoJSON(ST_GeomFromText('POINT(12.3456 23.4567)'),2,4) |
+------------------------------------------------------------+
| {"type": "Point", "coordinates": [12.35, 23.46]}            |
+------------------------------------------------------------+
1 row in set (0.00 sec)

mysql> SELECT ST_AsGeoJSON(ST_GeomFromText('POINT(12.3456 23.4567)'),2,5);
+----------------------------------------------------------------------------+
| ST_AsGeoJSON(ST_GeomFromText('POINT(12.3456 23.4567)'),2,5)                |
+----------------------------------------------------------------------------+
| {"bbox": [12.35, 23.46, 12.35, 23.46], "type": "Point", "coordinates": [12.35, 23.46]}|
+----------------------------------------------------------------------------+
1 row in set (0.00 sec)
```

9

PHP's JSON Functions

PHP, a recursive acronym for PHP: Hypertext Preprocessor, is a very popular programming language that is the core of up to 80 percent of the Internet and has its own JSON functions. The question for developers is how to take advantage of what PHP offers for JSON and how best to use it with MySQL. PHP's JSON functions require UTF8MB4-encoded strings.

JSON_DECODE

The JSON_DECODE function is used to convert a JSON string into a PHP variable. The MySQL JSON functions have no analog.

Format: mixed json_decode (string $json [, bool $assoc = false [, int $depth = 512 [, int $options = 0]]]).

The first argument is the JSON-formatted string to be decoded. The second is a Boolean value (true or false) to set the returned data into an associative array. The third argument is a recursive depth limit set to 1 or greater. The fourth and final argument has two settable options: JSON_OBJECT_AS_ARRAY, which has the same effect as setting $assoc to true, and JSON_BIGINT_AS_STRING, which casts big integers to strings instead of the default floats.

Example 9-1   *Simple PHP program to explore the PHP function JSON_DECODE*

```php
<?php

$json_string='{"name":"Dave","height":1.95,"c":[1,2,3]}';

var_dump(json_decode($json_string));            // Object output
var_dump(json_decode($json_string,true));    // Associative array
?>
```

Example 9-2   *Output of sample PHP program from Example 9-1*

```
php j1.php
object(stdClass)#1 (3) {
  ["name"]=>
  string(4) "Dave"
  ["height"]=>
  float(1.95)
  ["c"]=>
  array(3) {
    [0]=>
    int(1)
    [1]=>
    int(2)
    [2]=>
    int(3)
  }
}
```

```
array(3) {
  ["name"]=>
  string(4) "Dave"
  ["height"]=>
  float(1.95)
  ["c"]=>
  array(3) {
    [0]=>
    int(1)
    [1]=>
    int(2)
    [2]=>
    int(3)
  }
}
```

JSON_ENCODE

The JSON_ENCODE function turns values of variables into JSON strings:

```
string json_encode ( mixed $value [, int $options = 0 [, int $depth = 512 ]] )
```

10

Loading JSON Data

Although many JSON datasets are available, sometimes they are problematic to feed into a database. Often, at the start of a new programming project, a developer will be provided with some sample data that needs to be shoehorned onto the server, usually with little guidance other than "just get it on the server." This chapter offers some examples of how to do just that.

From Download to Database

Our first example involves a list of US postal, or ZIP, codes. It can be downloaded from http://jsonstudio.com/resources/ and it is free. (There are other similar datasets available that could use the same steps.) Taking the data from a download and converting it into a useful database requires several steps that will be detailed in the pages to follow.

Step 1: Examine the Data

The data for this example is supplied in a file named zips.zip. To unpack it, use unzip zips.zip. This will produce a file named zips.json. Example 10-1 shows the first rows of the file.

Example 10-1 *Examining the first rows of the zips.json datafile*

```
$ head zips.json
{ "city" : "AGAWAM", "loc" : [ -72.622739, 42.070206 ], "pop" : 15338, "state" : "MA", "_id" : "01001" }
{ "city" : "CUSHMAN", "loc" : [ -72.51564999999999, 42.377017 ], "pop" : 36963, "state" : "MA", "_id" : "01002" }
{ "city" : "BARRE", "loc" : [ -72.10835400000001, 42.409698 ], "pop" : 4546, "state" : "MA", "_id" : "01005" }
{ "city" : "BELCHERTOWN", "loc" : [ -72.41095300000001, 42.275103 ], "pop" : 10579, "state" : "MA", "_id" : "01007" }
{ "city" : "BLANDFORD", "loc" : [ -72.936114, 42.182949 ], "pop" : 1240, "state" : "MA", "_id" : "01008" }
{ "city" : "BRIMFIELD", "loc" : [ -72.188455, 42.116543 ], "pop" : 3706, "state" : "MA", "_id" : "01010" }
{ "city" : "CHESTER", "loc" : [ -72.988761, 42.279421 ], "pop" : 1688, "state" : "MA", "_id" : "01011" }
{ "city" : "CHESTERFIELD", "loc" : [ -72.833309, 42.38167 ], "pop" : 177, "state" : "MA", "_id" : "01012" }
{ "city" : "CHICOPEE", "loc" : [ -72.607962, 42.162046 ], "pop" : 23396, "state" : "MA", "_id" : "01013" }
{ "city" : "CHICOPEE", "loc" : [ -72.576142, 42.176443 ], "pop" : 31495, "state" : "MA", "_id" : "01020" }
```

The file contains almost 30,000 lines, with one record per line. Before you load all those lines into the server, it helps to determine some of the uses of that information. For illustration purposes, suppose we need to create a datafile in which a user entering a five-digit ZIP code would have city and state values returned. Or a user could enter a city and state set of values and receive the ZIP code.

But what does the data provide to us? It includes fields for city, loc, pop, state, and _id (which is the ZIP code itself). It makes sense to use _id as a primary key.

Step 2: Create the Table

ZIP codes require five numbers in length and some have a leading zero. MySQL's INT fields will drop any leading zeros, but CHAR fields will not. In this case, the leading zeros need to be retained because they are important, so a CHAR field will be used.

Example 10-2   *Creating a table for the JSON data*

```
mysql> use test;
Database changed
mysql> create table zipcode (doc JSON,
    _id char(5) GENERATED ALWAYS AS (JSON_UNQUOTE(JSON_EXTRACT(doc,'$._id')))
STORED NOT NULL,
    PRIMARY KEY (_id));
Query OK, 0 rows affected (0.03 sec)

mysql>
```

Step 3: Load the Data Using a Wrapper

Data often needs some tinkering to enable it to be imported into a database—even a schemaless database. We need a way to wrap each line of data into a SQL INSERT statement. This can be done with a very simple BASH script, as shown in Example 10-3.

Example 10-3   *BASH script file to wrap the individual lines of zips.json with a SQL statement*

```
#!/bin/bash
file="/home/dstokes/Downloads/zips.json"
while IFS= read line
do
       echo "INSERT INTO zipcode (doc) VALUES ('$line');"
done <"$file"
```

This script reads the data from the zips.json file, line by line, and then echoes the content wrapped in a SQL statement. This script can have its output piped to a MySQL session or sent to a file, as shown in Example 10-4.

Example 10-4   *Using the script from Example 10-3 to create a file with the generated SQL statements*

```
./loader.sh > foo
```

You can see in Example 10-5 that the data is now in a proper format for inserting into the database.

Example 10-5   *The first several lines of the output of the shell script, after transformation*

```
$head foo
INSERT INTO zipcode (doc) VALUES ('{ "city" : "AGAWAM", "loc" : [ -72.622739, 42.070206 ], "pop" : 15338,
"state" : "MA", "_id" : "01001" }');
INSERT INTO zipcode (doc) VALUES ('{ "city" : "CUSHMAN", "loc" : [ -72.51564999999999, 42.377017 ], "pop" :
36963, "state" : "MA", "_id" : "01002" }');
```

```
INSERT INTO zipcode (doc) VALUES ('{ "city" : "BARRE", "loc" : [ -72.10835400000001, 42.409698 ], "pop" : 4546,
"state" : "MA", "_id" : "01005" }');
INSERT INTO zipcode (doc) VALUES ('{ "city" : "BELCHERTOWN", "loc" : [ -72.41095300000001, 42.275103 ], "pop" :
10579, "state" : "MA", "_id" : "01007" }');
INSERT INTO zipcode (doc) VALUES ('{ "city" : "BLANDFORD", "loc" : [ -72.936114, 42.182949 ], "pop" : 1240,
"state" : "MA", "_id" : "01008" }');
INSERT INTO zipcode (doc) VALUES ('{ "city" : "BRIMFIELD", "loc" : [ -72.188455, 42.116543 ], "pop" : 3706,
"state" : "MA", "_id" : "01010" }');
INSERT INTO zipcode (doc) VALUES ('{ "city" : "CHESTER", "loc" : [ -72.988761, 42.279421 ], "pop" : 1688,
"state" : "MA", "_id" : "01011" }');
INSERT INTO zipcode (doc) VALUES ('{ "city" : "CHESTERFIELD", "loc" : [ -72.833309, 42.38167 ], "pop" : 177,
"state" : "MA", "_id" : "01012" }');
INSERT INTO zipcode (doc) VALUES ('{ "city" : "CHICOPEE", "loc" : [ -72.607962, 42.162046 ], "pop" : 23396,
"state" : "MA", "_id" : "01013" }');
INSERT INTO zipcode (doc) VALUES ('{ "city" : "CHICOPEE", "loc" : [ -72.576142, 42.176443 ], "pop" : 31495,
"state" : "MA", "_id" : "01020" }');
```

Finally, we can load the data with a simple `mysql -u root -p test < foo` command.

Step 4: Double-Check the Data

At this point, the data needs to be checked for quality. A good place to start is with the first record in the datafile to determine whether the data is complete. For ZIP codes, leading zeros are important and must be retained, so checking for an example with a leading zero assures that this was completed correctly.

Example 10-6   *Examining a known good example from the database*

```
mysql> select * from zipcode where _id = '01001';
+------------------------------------------------------------------------------+-------+
| doc                                                                          | _id   |
+------------------------------------------------------------------------------+-------+
| {"_id": "01001", "loc": [-72.622739, 42.070206], "pop": 15338, "city": "AGAWAM", "state": "MA"} | 01001 |
+------------------------------------------------------------------------------+-------+
1 row in set (0.00 sec)
```

Compare the first line in both the raw data and the foo file to ensure that they contain the same data. Then check the data in the database table. This also provides a way for you to check that the leading zero for the `_id` field has not been stripped (which would have occurred if an `INT` been used instead of a `CHAR` data type).

But what about looking up a ZIP code of a given a city and a state?

Example 10-7 *Finding the ZIP code given the city and state fields*

```
mysql> SELECT _id FROM zipcode
    -> WHERE JSON_EXTRACT(doc,"$.city") = "LEMON GROVE" AND
    -> JSON_EXTRACT(doc,"$.state") = "CA";
+-------+
| _id   |
+-------+
| 91945 |
+-------+
1 row in set (0.02 sec)
```

Many other validations can be performed on the data to spot-check the validity of the information, but the first tests are a good idea. From this point, you could take other steps to ease access of the data, such as using generated columns, views, stored procedures, or indexes on the data for future queries that are known to be desired at this point in development.

jq: JSON CLI Parser

Another option is the jq, a lightweight and flexible command-line JSON processor. This processor acts much like sed in that it enables you to slice, filter, map, and transform data from one format to another. For instance, it can be used to convert JSON data into CSV (comma-separated values) for loading into a non-JSON–columned MySQL database. You can download it from https://stedolan.github.io/jq/, and there is an online version at https://jqplay.org/ for experimentation. Plus, jq uses the Perl Compatible Regular Expressions (PCRE) parser, like many other languages. (This wonderful tool deserves to have much more written about it than the simple examples here, and reading the manual is a quick way to become acquainted with the many features of this tool.)

With No Arguments

With no arguments to jq, it will "pretty print" the JSON document. This is very handy for extremely complex documents with many layers of embedded objects and arrays that are hard to view on a single flat line.

Example 10-8 *Using jq without arguments will "pretty print" the JSON document.*

```
$ head -2 zips.json | jq
{
  "city": "AGAWAM",
  "loc": [
    -72.622739,
    42.070206
  ],
  "pop": 15338,
  "state": "MA",
  "_id": "01001"
}
{
  "city": "CUSHMAN",
  "loc": [
    -72.51565,
    42.377017
  ],
  "pop": 36963,
  "state": "MA",
  "_id": "01002"
}
```

Select Certain Fields

On some occasions, not all the data in a JSON document will be of interest, and you can use jq to reform the data and provide only selected parts.

Example 10-9 *Using jq to output only some of the data from the source JSON document*

```
$ head -2 zips.json | jq '{city, state, _id}'
{
  "city": "AGAWAM",
  "state": "MA",
  "_id": "01001"
}
{
  "city": "CUSHMAN",
  "state": "MA",
  "_id": "01002"
}
```

In Example 10-10, the value of the city key is converted into a value. Then that new key is given the value of the state key/value pair. The flexibility of jq can be a great asset.

Example 10-10   *Modifying the data to convert a key into a value*

```
$ head -2 zips.json | jq '{(.city): .state, _id}'
{
  "AGAWAM": "MA",
  "_id": "01001"
}
{
  "CUSHMAN": "MA",
  "_id": "01002"
}
```

The Restaurant Collection

MongoDB proved to be a popular NoSQL document store, and one of its example datasets is known as the *restaurant collection*. It is 25,359 lines of restaurant data that provides a good example for showing how to load data into MySQL. The entire collection can be downloaded from the URL listed in the appendix of this book.

First, notice that there is no _id key/value pair, unlike the ZIP code example. There is, however, a restaurant_id key/value pair that is unique for all the records. With working with InnoDB tables, it helps for you to have a primary key index of your choice. So the restaurant_id is an easy choice for use as a primary key.

Each line of this collection is a JSON object, bounded by curly brackets. Using a script similar to Example 10-3 to load the data seems like a good idea; however, this creates a problem in the data. Many of the records include apostrophes in the restaurant name, which will cause those records to fail with a SQL error—anything after the second apostrophe fails the syntax checker. To fix this, we need to change the single quote (') to a double single quote (''), which the server interprets as a properly escaped single quote in the middle of a literal. There are many ways of doing this, including using a favorite text editor. But large source files may be beyond the size that a text editor can handle. Linux users can use a stream editor such as sed. Once the single quotes are turned into double single quotes, the data can be fed into the server.

In Example 10-11, the data highlighted in bold italics shows what the MySQL syntax checker will actually check. The apostrophe in Kenny's will cause the checker to stop checking the SQL query. To fix this, we'd need to change Kenny's to Kenny''s so that the MySQL server would correctly escape the apostrophe in the name.

Example 10-11   *The syntax checker will check data up to the apostrophe in the word "Kenny's," but the apostrophe will stop the checker in its tracks.*

```
INSERT INTO restaurant (doc) values ('{"address": {"building": "1924", "coord":
[-73.9483236, 40.6387106], "street": "Nostrand Avenue", "zipcode": "11226"},
"borough": "Brooklyn", "cuisine": "Chinese", "grades": [{"date": {"$date":
1414368000000}, "grade": "A", "score": 7}, {"date": {"$date": 1384732800000},
"grade": "A", "score": 7}, {"date": {"$date": 1362528000000}, "grade": "B",
"score": 16}, {"date": {"$date": 1340668800000}, "grade": "A", "score": 9},
{"date": {"$date": 1326153600000}, "grade": "A", "score": 10}], "name": "Kenny's
Restaurant", "restaurant_id": "40919894"}');
```

One of the many commands that we could use is `sed`. The `sed` utility is a stream editor from the early days of the UNIX operating system. It is easy to tell it to search for single, single quotes and turn them into two single quotes.

Example 10-12   *Here, sed is used to convert single, single quotes into double single quotes.*

```
sed "s/'/''/g" primer-dataset.json > updated.json
```

Then we can use updated data with the loader script to create a table to feed to the database. This type of data cleaning is typical of what is needed to load third-party data into a database server.

Example 10-13   *The example record after the data has been cleaned up and then fed into the server*

```
mysql> SELECT _id, JSON_PRETTY(doc)  FROM restaurant LIMIT 1\G
*************************** 1. row ***************************
             _id: 30075445
JSON_PRETTY(doc): {
  "name": "Morris Park Bake Shop",
  "grades": [
    {
      "date": {
        "$date": 1393804800000
      },
      "grade": "A",
      "score": 2
    },
    {
      "date": {
        "$date": 1378857600000
      },
      "grade": "A",
      "score": 6
    },
```

```
    {
      "date": {
        "$date": 1358985600000
      },
      "grade": "A",
      "score": 10
    },
    {
      "date": {
        "$date": 1322006400000
      },
      "grade": "A",
      "score": 9
    },
    {
      "date": {
        "$date": 1299715200000
      },
      "grade": "B",
      "score": 14
    }
  ],
  "address": {
    "coord": [
      -73.856077,
      40.848447
    ],
    "street": "Morris Park Ave",
    "zipcode": "10462",
    "building": "1007"
  },
  "borough": "Bronx",
  "cuisine": "Bakery",
  "restaurant_id": "30075445"
}
1 row in set (0.00 sec)

mysql>
```

11

The MySQL Document Store

The MySQL JSON data type is extremely flexible. It may be a temptation for some to use the MySQL JSON data type by itself to provide an easy-to-use, schemaless data storage option. Simply having a table with one column, and that column being of type JSON, would be a very simple solution. Each row could have up to 1GB of JSON data. This idea is very close to the premise of the MySQL Document Store.

The MySQL JSON data type is the foundation of the MySQL Document Store. Relational databases need schemas and columns defined in tables before they can be used. But a document database enables developers to start saving and using data without having predefined data structures. As the data needed evolves for a given application, there is no need to call in a database administrator to redefine tables.

JSON provides for embedded arrays and objects and is a viable solution when the data does not fit into the relational model. There is also no need for an object relational mapping layer to map objects in a modern programming language to a column in a table. And this eliminates the need to embed a string with a Structured Query Language query in a program.

Having the document store built on the JSON data type enables you to use the same data as a document database or as a relational database—at the same time. And you can access collections and tables.

This chapter provides a general introduction to the MySQL Document Store, though this subject is deserving of its own book (or several). Refer to the MySQL documentation for full details.

By default, the MySQL Document Store creates two columns, doc and _id, as per most of the examples in this book. The InnoDB storage engine requires a primary key, and the _id field provides it. You can, of course, create your own collections with your own primary key.

The X DevAPI

MySQL engineers created the new X Protocol to provide functionality that the old MySQL protocol lacks. But what are some of the differences? The first is the network connection. Where the traditional protocol listened to TCP/IP port 3306, the new X Protocol listens to port 33060. The X Protocol has a new session model that enables code to scale from a single server to multiple servers. And the new protocol requires the use of a new shell—mysqlsh.

mysqlsh

The new mysqlsh shell is in some ways similar to the old mysql shell (better known as the MySQL Command Line Interface [CLI]), but in other ways it is a major leap forward. The interface is very similar and familiar, but it offers so much more. It is built upon the new X DevAPI, has multiple modes, and includes built-in language interpreters for JavaScript and Python. And it can also process Structured Query Language. The new API enables applications to scale easily from single to multiple server environments, and it provides nonblocking asynchronous calls common to many common host languages. The new shell was also designed for server administration for services such as InnoDB Cluster. To invoke this program, enter **mysqlsh**.

The X DevAPI session is a higher-level database session idea than the traditional lower-level MySQL connections. With X DevAPI, sessions can have several MySQL connections and can use either the classic MySQL protocol or the new X Protocol. The `ClassicSession` class provides a low-level MySQL connection to a single MySQL server instance. Applications taking advantage of the new features in the X DevAPI `NodeSession` class can be run against one server or a group of MySQL servers without code changes. The `NodeSession` class provides full support of X DevAPI but limited support of SQL.

After you've installed the new shell, enter **mysqlsh** to start—actually, enter **mysqlsh** *user@host*/**world_x**, using the actual username and hostname. In Example 11-1, the document with the `_id` equal to USA is specifically requested. Compare the example's syntax to the SQL equivalent `SELECT doc FROM countryinfo WHERE doc->"$._id" = 'USA';`.

Example 11-1 *Using the mysqlsh shell to access the MySQL Document Store to find a record in the countryinfo collection from the world_x sample database*

```
MySQL [localhost+/world_x] JS> db.countryinfo.find('_id = "USA"');
[
    {
        "GNP": 8510700,
        "IndepYear": 1776,
        "Name": "United States",
        "_id": "USA",
        "demographics": {
            "LifeExpectancy": 77.0999984741211,
            "Population": 278357000
        },
        "geography": {
            "Continent": "North America",
            "Region": "North America",
            "SurfaceArea": 9363520
        },
        "government": {
            "GovernmentForm": "Federal Republic",
            "HeadOfState": "George W. Bush"
        }
    }
]
1 document in set (0.00 sec)
MySQL [localhost+/world_x] JS>
```

The new shell has three modes—Python, JavaScript, and SQL—and acts very similarly to the old shell, especially when in SQL mode. In the example, JavaScript mode is in use, as indicated by the `JS>` prompt. In some of the following examples, the mode is switched to SQL mode.

Connections

The MySQL mysqlsh shell features the ability to connect using the classic MySQL protocol and the new X DevAPI protocol. Specifics for the connections use a Uniform Resource Identifier (URI). X protocol connections are TCP only, while the classic protocol tries to default to UNIX sockets.

The URI can be specified on the line starting the shell, such as `mysqlsh -uri user:password@host:33060/schema`, or you can simply start the shell and then connect with `\connect user@host/schema` (assuming you want to be prompted for the password and the MySQL server is listening to port 33060).

Session Types

There are two types of sessions under the new MySQL mysqlsh shell. `NodeSession` is designed for new applications with MySQL servers that support the X DevAPI protocol (MySQL 5.7.12 or more recent), and the `ClassicSession` is for servers without the X Protocol. All the exciting CRUD (Create, Replace, Update, Delete) and newer features are available only with the `NodeSession`. At shell invocation, entering `-sqln` creates a `NodeSession`, while entering `-sqlc` creates a `ClassicSession`.

After the shell has been started, connections will attempt by default to use the X DevAPI protocol. In Example 11-2, user dstokes connects to the localhost to access the world_x schema.

Example 11-2 *Connecting after the MySQL mysqlsh shell has been started.*

```
MySQL Shell 8.0.3-labs
Copyright (c) 2016, 2017, Oracle and/or its affiliates. All rights reserved.
Oracle is a registered trademark of Oracle Corporation and/or its affiliates.
Other names may be trademarks of their respective owners.
Type '\help' or '\?' for help; '\quit' to exit.
```

```
MySQL JS> \connect dstokes@localhost/world_x
Creating a session to 'dstokes@localhost/world_x'
Enter password: ******
Your MySQL connection id is 5 (X protocol)
Server version: 5.7.20-log MySQL Community Server (GPL)
Default schema 'world_x' accessible through db.
Fetching schema names for auto-completion... Press ^C to stop.
MySQL [localhost+/world_x] JS> session
<Session:dstokes@localhost/world_x>
MySQL [localhost+/world_x] JS>

$ mysqlsh root@localhost/world_x
Creating a session to 'root@localhost/world_x'
Enter password: ******
Your MySQL connection id is 8 (X protocol)
Server version: 8.0.3-rc-log MySQL Community Server (GPL)
Default schema 'world_x' accessible through db.
Fetching schema names for auto-completion... Press ^C to stop.
```

Example 11-3   *Connecting with the connection specifics on the command line*

```
MySQL Shell 8.0.3-labs
Copyright (c) 2016, 2017, Oracle and/or its affiliates. All rights reserved.
Oracle is a registered trademark of Oracle Corporation and/or its affiliates.
Other names may be trademarks of their respective owners.
Type '\help' or '\?' for help; '\quit' to exit.

 MySQL  localhost:33060+ ssl  world_x  JS >
```

Once you have invoked the shell and logged in, you are ready to get to work.

Collections and Documents

Documents are stored in collections. Collections are containers for documents that hopefully share a purpose. It is easy to create a new collection. Ignoring the details of the new mysqlsh shell commands for the moment, Example 11-4 uses the schema test as the working document. The session has already been created (the user already logged in to the server). And the object named db is a global variable assigned to the current active schema. The third bolded command, db.createCollection('demo'), does the actual creation of a new document collection named demo. Lastly, the get-Collections() function shows the available collections.

Example 11-4   *This example shows connecting to the test schema, referenced as the object db, and then creating a collection named demo.*

```
MySQL [localhost+/world_x] JS> \use test
Default schema 'test' accessible through db.
```

```
MySQL [localhost+/test] JS> db
<Schema:test>
MySQL [localhost+/test] JS> db.createCollection('demo')
<Collection:demo>
MySQL [localhost+/test] JS> db.getCollections();
[
    <Collection:demo>,
    <Collection:foo>
]
MySQL [localhost+/test] JS>
```

In Example 11-4, \use test tells the server which schema to use. The server uses db as a pointer object to point to the chosen schema, and issuing db by itself confirms it is the selected schema. Next is a collection with the name of demo. And, finally, the getCollections() function reports any available collections in the test schema. This is using MySQL without the SQL.

Behind the scenes, the MySQL server has created the desired collection. To see the work performed is a very simple matter; at the mysqlsh prompt, you enter the SQL mode by entering \sql. Note the prompt will change to mysql-sh>. From here on, until the shell is exited or the mode is changed again, traditional SQL commands are accepted.

Example 11-5 *Collection created by db.createCollection('demo') as viewed from the SQL side of the server*

```
MySQL [localhost+/test] JS> \sql
Switching to SQL mode... Commands end with ;
MySQL [localhost+/test] SQL> DESC demo;
+--------+-------------+------+-----+---------+-------------------+
| Field  | Type        | Null | Key | Default | Extra             |
+--------+-------------+------+-----+---------+-------------------+
| doc    | json        | YES  |     | NULL    |                   |
| _id    | varchar(32) | NO   | PRI | NULL    | STORED GENERATED  |
+--------+-------------+------+-----+---------+-------------------+
2 rows in set (0.01 sec)
MySQL [localhost+/test] SQL>
```

A JSON column named doc and a VARCHAR column named _id were automatically generated when the collection was created. A table named demo has been created with two columns. The first column is named doc and is in the JSON data type. The second column is a varchar named _id that is a stored generated column. You can see more details by using the SHOW CREATE TABLE demo command.

Example 11-6 *More details of the demo collection providing details on how the _id column was created by the use of a generated column*

```
MySQL [localhost+/test] SQL> SHOW CREATE TABLE demo;
+--------+-----------------------------------------------------------+
| Table  | Create Table                                              |
+--------+-----------------------------------------------------------+
| demo   | CREATE TABLE 'demo' (
  'doc' json DEFAULT NULL,
  '_id' varchar(32) GENERATED ALWAYS AS
    (json_unquote(json_extract('doc','$._id'))) STORED NOT NULL,
  PRIMARY KEY ('_id')
) ENGINE=InnoDB DEFAULT CHARSET=utf8mb4 |
+--------+-----------------------------------------------------------+
1 row in set (0.00 sec)
MySQL [localhost+/test] SQL>
```

The _id column is generated by extracting and unquoting the _id key (with the use of JSON_EXTRACT and JSON_UNQUOTE) from the JSON document and placing that data in the column. This should be very familiar if you read Chapter 7 on generated columns. Note that the document store will generate a value for the _id value if one is not specified; specifying your own _id will require a string, not a number—that is, "10" not 10. And having _id designated as the primary key fulfills the need of the InnoDB storage engine to have a primary key.

CRUD: Create, Replace, Update, Delete

The MySQL Document Store provides functions for CRUD operations (Create, Replace, Update, and Delete) for documents in a collection: add(), modify(), and remove(). These three functions, when combined with find(), are the core basic operations most developers need on an ongoing basis to take advantage of the document database.

In Example 11-7, note that _id is defined as a VARCHAR(32) and the number "101" has to be a string in quotes. Note the use of \js to switch to JavaScript mode from SQL mode.

Example 11-7 *Adding a document to a collection*

```
MySQL [localhost+/test] SQL> \js
Switching to JavaScript mode...
MySQL [localhost+/test] JS> db.demo.add({"_id" : "101"})
Query OK, 1 item affected (0.01 sec)
MySQL [localhost+/test] JS> db.demo.find()
```

```
[
    {
        "_id": "101"
    }
]
1 document in set (0.00 sec)
MySQL [localhost+/test] JS>
```

The documents in a collection can be acted upon very easily and by a number of functions. These functions have various ways to improve queries. In Example 11-8, the top or root object is extended with the key/value pair of shoe and 50. Besides objects, arrays can be added to the document.

Example 11-8 *Using set to modify a document by adding another key/value pair*

```
MySQL [localhost+/test] JS> db.demo.modify("_id='101'").set("shoe",50)
Query OK, 1 item affected (0.01 sec)
MySQL [localhost+/test] JS> db.demo.find("_id='101'")
[
    {
        "_id": "101",
        "shoe": 50
    }
]
1 document in set (0.00 sec)
```

You can also add an array value to a document.

Example 11-9 *Adding an array value to a document*

```
MySQL [localhost+/test] JS> db.demo.modify("_id='101'").
set("feet","[left,right]
")
Query OK, 1 item affected (0.01 sec)
MySQL [localhost+/test] JS> db.demo.find("_id='101'")
[
    {
        "_id": "101",
        "feet": "[left,right]",
        "shoe": 50
    }
]
1 document in set (0.00 sec)
MySQL [localhost+/test] JS>
```

Arrays can also be added to a document with set. Note that the particular _id to be modified has been specified in Example 11-10. Without denoting the exact record to be modified, *all* the documents in the collection would be modified.

Example 11-10 *Removing a key/value pair from a document*

```
MySQL [localhost+/test] JS> db.demo.modify("_id='101'").unset("feet")
Query OK, 1 item affected (0.01 sec)
MySQL [localhost+/test] JS> db.demo.find("_id='101'")
[
    {
        "_id": "101",
        "shoe": 50
    }
]
1 document in set (0.00 sec)
MySQL [localhost+/test] JS>
```

The unset() function requires only the name of the key of the key/value pair to be deleted. Note in Example 11-10 the use of the "_id='101'" qualifier in the modify() function to specify the exact document to be modified; omission of a way to find the *exact* document to be modified will result in *all* the records in the collection being affected.

NOTE   *Be sure to back up your critical data. Retyping documents is laborious, boring, and unproductive.*

Arrays can be appended very easily with arrayAppend, and it will append to the end of the array at the key. In Example 11-11, the key feet now has two arrays for values associated with it. To append the array [toes,arch,heel,ankle] to the first array, modify the path from $.feet to $.feet[0] and the result will be [left,right,toe,arch,heel,ankle] if you want both combined.

Example 11-11 *Adding and then appending an array to a document*

```
MySQL [localhost+/test] JS> db.demo.modify("_id='101'").set("feet","[left,right]
")
Query OK, 1 item affected (0.01 sec)
MySQL [localhost+/test] JS> db.demo.modify("_id='101'").arrayAppend('$.feet',
"[toe,arch,heel,ankle]")
Query OK, 1 item affected (0.01 sec)
MySQL [localhost+/test] JS> db.demo.find("_id='101'")
[
    {
        "_id": "101",
        "feet": [
            "[left,right]",
            "[toe,arch,heel,ankle]"
        ],
        "shoe": 50
    }
]
1 document in set (0.00 sec)
MySQL [localhost+/test] JS>
```

Finally, documents can be removed with the `remove()` function. Remember to specify the record or records desired for deletion, or *all* the documents in the collection will head for the bit bucket.

Example 11-12 *Removing* one *record that matches*

```
MySQL [localhost+/test] JS> db.demo.remove("_id='101'")
Query OK, 1 item affected (0.01 sec)
MySQL [localhost+/test] JS> db.demo.find()
Empty set (0.00 sec)
MySQL [localhost+/test] JS>
```

The `add()` function can accept valid JSON-formatted documents on a single or on multiple lines. Example 11-13 shows the entry of two records on multiple lines.

Example 11-13 *Adding records*

```
MySQL [localhost+/test] JS> db.demo.add(
                         -> {
                         -> _id : "101",
                         -> first : "Moe",
                         -> last : "Howard"
                         -> }
                         -> )
                         ->
Query OK, 1 item affected (0.01 sec)
MySQL [localhost+/test] JS> db.demo.add(
                         -> {
                         -> _id : "201",
                         -> first : "Shemp",
                         -> last : "Howard"
                         -> }
                         -> )
                         ->
Query OK, 1 item affected (0.00 sec)
MySQL [localhost+/test] JS>
```

Filtering Find

The `find()` function can be tuned to narrow searches or select only certain fields.

Example 11-14 *The find() function can be modified to narrow down searches and to specify only certain parts of the document are in the returned data.*

```
MySQL [localhost+/test] JS> db.demo.find("last = 'Fine' OR _id = '41'")
[
    {
        "_id": "33",
        "first": "Larry",
        "last": "Fine"
    },
    {
        "_id": "41",
        "first": "Curly",
        "last": "Howard"
    }
]
2 documents in set (0.00 sec)
MySQL [localhost+/test] JS> db.demo.find().fields(["first","last"])
[
    {
        "first": "Moe",
        "last": "Howard"
    },
    {
        "first": "Shemp",
        "last": "Howard"
    },
    {
        "first": "Larry",
        "last": "Fine"
    },
    {
        "first": "Curly",
        "last": "Howard"
    }
]
4 documents in set (0.00 sec)
MySQL [localhost+/test] JS>
```

The limit() and skip() functions can also help winnow down returned data.

Example 11-15 *Using the limit() and skip() functions to winnow down returned data*

```
MySQL [localhost+/test] JS> db.demo.find().limit(2)
[
    {
        "_id": "101",
        "first": "Moe",
        "last": "Howard"
    },
```

```
    {
        "_id": "201",
        "first": "Shemp",
        "last": "Howard"
    }
]
2 documents in set (0.00 sec)
MySQL [localhost+/test] JS> db.demo.find().limit(2).skip(1)
[
    {
        "_id": "201",
        "first": "Shemp",
        "last": "Howard"
    },
    {
        "_id": "33",
        "first": "Larry",
        "last": "Fine"
    }
]
2 documents in set (0.00 sec)
MySQL [localhost+/test] JS>
```

Sorting

The sort() function can be postpended to find() to order the returned
document. But sort() requires that one or more fields in the document be
named as a key. With a key named to sort upon, the server will send back an
"Invalid number of arguments in CollectionFind.sort, expected at least 1 but
got 0 (ArgumentError)" error message. If you also use the fields() function, you need to specify one or more of the returned document keys as the
field on which to sort. Omitting the field name to be sorted will result in an
"Illegal number of arguments" error message.

Example 11-16 *Sorting can be done, but the fields need to be specified to be passed
to the sort() function.*

```
MySQL [localhost+/test] JS> db.demo.find().fields(["last","first"]).
sort("first")
[
    {
        "first": "Curly",
        "last": "Howard"
    },
    {
        "first": "Larry",
        "last": "Fine"
```

```
    },
    {
        "first": "Moe",
        "last": "Howard"
    },
    {
        "first": "Shemp",
        "last": "Howard"
    }
]
4 documents in set (0.00 sec)
MySQL [localhost+/test] JS>
```

If fields are not specified, you can use any key in the document for the sort key.

Example 11-17   *Using any key in the document for the sort key*

```
MySQL [localhost+/test] JS> db.demo.find().sort("_id")
[
    {
        "_id": "101",
        "first": "Moe",
        "last": "Howard"
    },
    {
        "_id": "201",
        "first": "Shemp",
        "last": "Howard"
    },
    {
        "_id": "33",
        "first": "Larry",
        "last": "Fine"
    },
    {
        "_id": "41",
        "first": "Curly",
        "last": "Howard"
    }
]
4 documents in set (0.00 sec)
```

Binding

Binding values to variables is also possible and highly desirable in scripts when iterating over values. In Example 11-18, a variable is declared by prepending a colon (:) to the name of the variable. The bind() function then replaces the variable with the value before executing the command.

Example 11-18 *Passing bound parameters*

```
MySQL [localhost+/test] JS> db.demo.find("last = :lastname").bind("lastname","Fine")
[
    {
        "_id": "33",
        "first": "Larry",
        "last": "Fine"
    }
]
1 document in set (0.00 sec)
MySQL [localhost+/test] JS>
```

Indexing Collections

Indexes may be added to speed up the process of finding specific documents in a MySQL Document Store, just like in the "regular old MySQL relational server." Indexes enable the server to go directly to the record or records desired without having to process every record in the collection. Processing every record is better known as a *full table scan,* and database administrators work hard to eliminate full scans. Sometimes your application does need to read through all the records in a collection—for processing all the accounts payables, for example—but generally full scans are to be avoided. Generally, we don't need to read the entire computer manual to find an answer to a single question when the manual has an index that we can use to look up the answer.

Indexes are not a panacea for databases, however. Indexes are a separate table that needs to be read, maintained as records change or are removed, and managed. It is often tempting to novice database developers to index all columns, but the overhead of doing this can greatly slow operations.

Indexes are generally unique or not. Unique indexes will have a pointer to one record in the collection. Nonunique indexes can have multiple entries. Consider a billing system where each customer will have its own unique identification number, but the order collection will hold the identification number of multiple customers.

Example 11-19 *Creating indexes*

```
MySQL [localhost+/test] JS> db.demo.createIndex("id_idx").
                         -> field("_id", "INTEGER",    false).execute()
                         ->
Query OK, 0 items affected (0.10 sec)
MySQL [localhost+/test] JS> \sql
```

```
Switching to SQL mode... Commands end with ;
MySQL [localhost+/test] SQL> DESC demo;
+------------------------------------------------+--------------+------+-----+---
------+-------------------+
| Field                                          | Type         | Null | Key | Default | Extra |
+------------------------------------------------+--------------+------+-----+---
------+-------------------+
| doc                                            | json         | YES  |     | NULL    |       |
| _id                                            | varchar(32)  | NO   | PRI | NULL    |       |
STORED GENERATED   |
| $ix_i_ED8EA5BF0D44065A674B92033FC24920B41C5F42 | int(11)      | YES  | MUL | NULL    |       |
VIRTUAL GENERATED  |
+------------------------------------------------+--------------+------+-----+---
------+-------------------+
3 rows in set (0.00 sec)
MySQL [localhost+/test] SQL> \js
Switching to JavaScript mode...
MySQL [localhost+/test] JS> db.demo.dropIndex("id_idx").execute()
Query OK, 0 rows affected (0.05 sec)
MySQL [localhost+/test] JS>
```

Note that the EXPLAIN command can be used in SQL mode, but not in Python or JavaScript.

Example 11-20 shows how to create a nonunique index, and Example 11-21 creates a unique index.

Example 11-20   *Creating a nonunique index*

```
mysql-js> db.demo.createIndex("last_idx").
field("last","TEXT(30)",false).execute()
Query OK (0.09 sec)
mysql-js>
```

Example 11-21   *Unique indexes can also be created, but the field values need to be unique.*

```
mysql-js> db.demo.createIndex("last_idx2",mysqlx.IndexType.UNIQUE).
field("last"
"TEXT(30)",true).execute()
Duplicate entry 'Howard' for key 'last_idx2' (MySQL Error 1062)
mysql-js>
```

If a unique index is created, any attempt at inserting a duplicate value will produce an error, as shown in Example 11-22. Sometimes this is caused when you try to add to a document that instead should be modified; other times this can result from carelessness. Often you will see MySQL relational tables use an AUTO_INCREMENT definer on a column to have unique values supplied for unique identifiers.

Example 11-22 *An error occurs if you attempt to insert a duplicate value.*

```
mysql-js> db.demo.createIndex("first_idx",mysqlx.IndexType.UNIQUE).field("first"
,"TEXT(30)",true).execute()
Query OK (0.20 sec)
mysql-js> db.demo.add(
    ... {
    ... _id : "401",
    ... first : "Moe",
    ... last : "Jones"
    ... }
    ... )
    ...
ERROR: 5116: Document contains a field value that is not unique but required to
be
mysql-js>
```

The MySQL Document Store will automatically add a unique _id key if you do not specify a value and use a generated column to build an index. The automatically generated _ids will look something like this: 3019886f8e6fd311640d4851b70943c6 or ac5a657d8e6fd311640d4851b70943c6. You can specify your own _id values (remember they are strings and need quotes around them) and use your own scheme for values.

Dropping a Collection

Data has a lifespan, and it is fairly simple to remove or drop a collection. The name of the schema and the name of the collection must be specified. Once data is dropped, you can recover the data only from a backup or by re-entering the data if you have a very good memory.

Example 11-23 *Removing the demo collection from the test schema*

```
mysql-js> db.getCollections()
[
    <Collection:demo>,
    <Collection:foo>
]
mysql-js> session.dropCollection("test","demo")
Query OK (0.03 sec)
mysql-js> db.getCollections()
[
    <Collection:foo>
]
mysql-js>
```

12

Programming with the MySQL Document Store

For decades, developers have needed to embed SQL as strings in their code or use object-relational mapping (ORM) to be able to use a database. The SQL strings are often esthetically objectionable, sitting in the middle of a beautifully constructed modern program written in a modern programming language. ORMs are often another complexity that can be avoided if developers would learn to write SQL properly. However, there is very little training in SQL, the relational model, or even set theory for most programmers. SQL is a powerful computer language, but very few attempt to master it, even if they seek high-performing queries.

Developers can use the MySQL Document Store from many programming languages without requiring embedded SQL strings, ORMs, or intensive study in relational databases. It takes away the esthetic complaints and enables those without SQL skills to use the power of MySQL.

The X DevAPI includes connectors for most languages. The big change that programmers will quickly notice is that there are no messy strings of SQL queries in the code. Much of the approach is the same as the traditional programming methodology—authentication to server, designating a schema, issuing a query, and returning the results—but the code looks much cleaner.

As of this writing, MySQL provides connectors for Java (Connector/J), C++, Node.JS, .Net, and Python. A PHP Extension Community Library (PECL) extension for PHP is available. The MySQL connectors are available from the MySQL web site, and the PHP PECL extension is available from PECL.PHP.Net web site. More connectors may be available at a later date.

Programming Examples

Learning to program has a steep learning curve. Learning to program with a new paradigm can be as difficult. The MySQL Document Store is a big shift for those who are used to embedding SQL queries in strings in their code. Those who are starting to work with MySQL who never used embedded strings could find the steps in working with a database—connecting, authorization, linking up to a schema, query execution, and the return of the data—a strange new phenomena. To help ease both groups into working with the MySQL Document Store, the following simple programs are provided for the reader to copy and hopefully enhance.

Python Example

Example 12-1 is in Python but is a typical example of the coding style when using the X DevAPI.

Example 12-1 *Using the MySQL Document Store with the MySQL X DevAPI Python Connector*

```python
import mysqlx

# Connect to server on localhost
session = mysqlx.get_session({
    'host': 'localhost',
    'port': 33060,
    'user': 'dave',
    'password': 'S3cR3T!',
    'ssl-mode' : mysqlx.SSLMode.DISABLED #Remove this line if SSL enabled
})

schema = session.get_schema('world_x')

# Use the collection 'countryinfo'
collection = schema.get_collection('countryinfo')

# Specify which document to find with Collection.find()
result = collection.find('_id like :param').bind('param', 'USA').execute()

# Print document
docs = result.fetch_all()
print('id: {0}'.format(docs[0]['Name']))
```

Node.JS Example

Similar code in Node.JS will also seem very familiar to you after reading Chapter 11. The language differences between Node.JS and Python are still evident, but the X DevAPI code—getCollection(), find()—remains the same.

Example 12-2 *The equivalent code in Node.JS retains the familiar X DevAPI function calls and is very similar to the code written in Python in Example 12-1.*

```javascript
// Simple example to grab one record and print it
const mysqlx = require('@mysql/xdevapi');
const options = {
  host: 'localhost',
  port: 33060,
  dbUser: 'dave',
  dbPassword: 'S3cR3t!!'
};

mysqlx
  .getSession(options)
  .then (session => {
  var schema = session.getSchema('world_x');
```

```
//equivalent of SELECT doc FROM countryinfo where _id = 'USA'
  var coll = schema.getCollection('countryinfo');
  var query = "$._id == 'USA'";

      // Print doc
    return Promise.all([
      coll.find(query).execute(function (doc) {
      console.log(doc);
      }),
      session.close()
    ]);
  })
  .catch(err => {
      console.log(err.message);
      console.log(err.stack);
  });
```

PHP Example

PHP is a very popular web programming language, and once again the code
looks similar to previous examples.

Example 12-3 *The X DevAPI calls retain a familiar format despite the code now being
in PHP.*

```
#!/usr/bin/php
<?PHP
// Connection parameters
  $user = 'dave';
  $passwd = 'S3cR3t!';
  $host = 'localhost';
  $port = '33060';
  $connection_uri = 'mysqlx://'.$user.':'.$passwd.'@'.$host.':'.$port;
  echo $connection_uri . "\n";

// Connect as a Node Session
  $nodeSession = mysql_xdevapi\getNodeSession($connection_uri);
// "USE world_x"
  $schema = $nodeSession->getSchema("world_x");
// Specify collection to use
  $collection = $schema->getCollection("countryinfo");

// Query the Document Store
  $result = $collection->find('_id = "USA"')->fields(['Name as
Country','geography as Geo','geography.Region'])->execute();

// Fetch/Display data
  $data = $result->fetchAll();
  var_dump($data);
?>
```

Traditional SQL vs. MySQL Document Store

The MySQL Document Store also enables developers to choose between the traditional SQL approach and the MySQL Document Store approach. Example 12-4 shows the same PHP code in both formats.

Example 12-4 *The same program written in PHP with traditional SQL and MySQL Document Store*

Traditional SQL:

```
<?PHP
// Connection parameters
$host='127.0.0.1';
$user='dave';
$pass='S3cR3t!';
$db  = 'world_x';

// connect to database server
$mysqli = mysqli_connect('localhost','root','hidave');

// Choose schema
$mysqli->select_db('world_x');

// send SQL query

if ($result = $mysqli->query("SELECT doc FROM countryinfo WHERE _id='USA'")) {
    $row = mysqli_fetch_row($result);
    var_dump($row);
}
?>
```

Document Store:

```
<?PHP
// Connection parameters
  $user = 'dave';
  $passwd = 'S3cR3t!';
  $host = 'localhost';
  $port = '33060';

  $connection_uri = 'mysqlx://'.$user.':'.$passwd.'@'.$host.':'.$port;

// Connect as a Node Session
  $nodeSession = mysql_xdevapi\getNodeSession($connection_uri);

// Choose schema
  $schema = $nodeSession->getSchema("world_x");

// Specify collection to use
  $collection = $schema->getCollection("countryinfo");
  $result = $collection->find('_id = "USA"')->execute();
  $data = $result->fetchAll();
  var_dump($data);
?>
```

Developers can use the traditional SQL, the MySQL Document Store, or both. It would not be a good programming practice to combine both.

The MySQL Shell and JavaScript

The new MySQL Shell (mysqlsh) also has modes for JavaScript and Python. It is very easy to start up the shell and simply enter code. It is also very simple to use the built-in JavaScript or Python interpreters with the MySQL shell to store JSON documents or programmatically access data.

Example 12-5   *An example of using the JavaScript interpreter built into the MySQL shell programmatically*

```
MySQL Shell 1.0.11
Copyright (c) 2016, 2017, Oracle and/or its affiliates. All rights reserved.
Oracle is a registered trademark of Oracle Corporation and/or its Affiliates.
Other names may be trademarks of their respective owners.
Type '\help' or '\?' for help; '\quit' to exit.
Currently in JavaScript mode. Use \sql to switch to SQL mode and execute queries.

mysql-js> var mysqlx = require('mysqlx');
mysql-js> var mySession = mysqlx.getNodeSession( {
      ... host: 'localhost', port: 33060, dbUser : 'root', dbPassword : 'hidave'
});
      ...
mysql-js> var db = mySession.getSchema('test');
mysql-js> var foo = db.createCollection('foobarx');
mysql-js> foo.add({name : "Dave", location : "Texas"}).execute();
Query OK, 1 item affected (0.01 sec)
mysql-js>
mysql-js> var document = foo.find().execute();
mysql-js> print(document.fetchOne());
{
    "_id": "27190ac58976d31184064851b70943c6",
    "location": "Texas",
    "name": "Dave"
}
mysql-js>
```

Relational Tables

The MySQL Document Store can also be used to access relational tables or to treat collections as tables. The following examples use the world_x database and assume the user has connected successfully to the MySQL Server. The **db** object still refers to the schema selected.

Example 12-6 *Similar in fashion to addressing a collection, relational tables can be accessed from the MySQL Document Store.*

```
MySQL [localhost+/world_x] JS> db.city.select().limit(4);
+----+----------------+-------------+-----------+--------------------------+
| ID | Name           | CountryCode | District  | Info                     |
+----+----------------+-------------+-----------+--------------------------+
|  1 | Kabul          | AFG         | Kabol     | {"Population": 1780000}  |
|  2 | Qandahar       | AFG         | Qandahar  | {"Population": 237500}   |
|  3 | Herat          | AFG         | Herat     | {"Population": 186800}   |
|  4 | Mazar-e-Sharif | AFG         | Balkh     | {"Population": 127800}   |
+----+----------------+-------------+-----------+--------------------------+
4 rows in set (0.00 sec)
MySQL [localhost+/world_x] JS>
```

But collections and relational tables are not the same. Relational tables have their own set of functions.

Example 12-7 *The getTables() function is used to find relational tables, while getCollections() is used to find collections.*

```
MySQL [localhost+/world_x] JS> db.getTables();
[
    <Table:city>,
    <Table:country>,
    <Table:countrylanguage>
]
MySQL [localhost+/world_x] JS> db.getCollections();
[
    <Collection:countryinfo>
]
MySQL [localhost+/world_x] JS>
```

The relational functions for CRUD (Create, Replace, Update, and Delete) are named *insert()*, *select()*, *update()*, and *delete()*. These are analogous to their SQL commands.

Filtering commands are similar to the SQL commands.

Example 12-8 *Filtering queries for relational tables are similar to other MySQL Document Store features but look more like their SQL variants.*

```
MySQL [localhost+/world_x] JS> db.city.select("Name","District").
where("CountryCode = 'USA'").limit(4);
+-------------+------------+
| Name        | District   |
+-------------+------------+
| New York    | New York   |
| Los Angeles | California |
| Chicago     | Illinois   |
| Houston     | Texas      |
+-------------+------------+
4 rows in set (0.01 sec)
MySQL [localhost+/world_x] JS>
```

Both Relational and Document

It is possible to use the MySQL Document Store to access document data in relational tables. This is done very easily with the `->` operator or `JSON_EXTRACT()`.

Example 12-9 *This query shows how to extract JSON document data from a relational table.*

```
MySQL [localhost+/world_x] JS> db.city.select(["Name", "CountryCode", "District"
, "Info"]).   where("CountryCode = :country and Info->'$.Population' > 1000000")
.  bind('country', 'USA') ;
+-------------+-------------+--------------+------------------------+
| Name        | CountryCode | District     | Info                   |
+-------------+-------------+--------------+------------------------+
| New York    | USA         | New York     | {"Population": 8008278} |
| Los Angeles | USA         | California    | {"Population": 3694820} |
| Chicago     | USA         | Illinois     | {"Population": 2896016} |
| Houston     | USA         | Texas        | {"Population": 1953631} |
| Philadelphia| USA         | Pennsylvania | {"Population": 1517550} |
| Phoenix     | USA         | Arizona      | {"Population": 1321045} |
| San Diego   | USA         | California    | {"Population": 1223400} |
| Dallas      | USA         | Texas        | {"Population": 1188580} |
| San Antonio | USA         | Texas        | {"Population": 1144646} |
+-------------+-------------+--------------+------------------------+
9 rows in set (0.01 sec)
MySQL [localhost+/world_x] JS>
```

Document as Relational

To complete the treating of document data as relational data, the MySQL Document Store also provides the ability to cast documents as tables.

Example 12-10 *The countryinfo collection has been cast as a relational table, and the query treats the data as a relational table with JSON data inside.*

```
MySQL JS> var ci = db.getCollectionAsTable('countryinfo');
MySQL JS> var result = ci.select(["doc->'$.Name'"]).where("doc->'$._id' = 'USA'").execute();
MySQL JS> var data = result.fetchOne();
MySQL JS> print ("Name : " + data[0]);
Name : "United States"MySQL [localhost+/world_x] JS>
```

A

Additional Resources

Many developer resources are available to help you write code and experiment with MySQL and JSON. Google's Protocol Buffers, the world_x database, MySQL Labs software, JSON datasets, and more are available.

https://developers.google.com/protocol-buffers/ The MySQL X DevAPI relies on Google's Protocol Buffers, which are language- and platform-neutral methods you can use to define the storage of data. You can define the ways in which you can pass data, and the Protocol Buffer Compiler builds classes for use within programming languages. You can also make additions to the methods you use for passing data without losing backward-compatibility.

When compiling the X DevAPI code from source code, you will need to download and build the Google Protocol Buffer software. You may also need to build this code when using repackaged connectors. Prebuilt Google Protocol Buffer software may exist for the operating system of your choice. Refer to the web site for more information.

https://dev.mysql.com/doc/index-other.html   The world_x database is an evolution of the world database used by MySQL for decades in documentation, classes, and blogs.

https://labs.mysql.com/   From time to time, MySQL Labs offers an early glimpse into possible future software releases. This software is for *testing purposes only* and is *not* recommended for production. Treat it as a proof of concept and provide any feedback you can; the experimental code may not make it into production.

https://jsonstudio.com/resources/   You'll find many great example datasets in JSON to experiment with to help develop proficiency. The ZIP code data and other great sets are available here.

https://stedolan.github.io/jq/   The jq command-line JSON parser can be found here.

https://raw.githubusercontent.com/mongo/docs-assets/primer-dataset/ primer-dataset.json   Download the example MongoDB dataset here.

Index

Join the World's Largest Developer Community

 Download the latest software, tools, and developer templates

 Get exclusive access to hands-on trainings and workshops

 Grow your professional network through the Oracle ACE Program

 Publish your technical articles – and get paid to share your expertise

ORACLE DEVELOPER COMMUNITY developer.oracle.com
Membership is Free | Follow Us on Social:

🐦 @OracleDevs   f facebook.com/OracleDevs

Certification
MATTERS

72% Experienced a Greater Demand for Their Skills[1]

67% Said Certification was a Key Factor in Recent Raise[1]

64% Received Positive Impact on Professional Image[2]

Oracle University
Differentiate Yourself to Attract Employers

certification.oracle.com

Push a Button
Move Your Java Apps to the Oracle Cloud

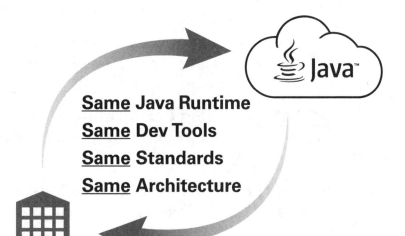

Same Java Runtime
Same Dev Tools
Same Standards
Same Architecture

... or Back to Your Data Center

ORACLE®

cloud.oracle.com/java
or call 1.800.ORACLE.1

Oracle Learning Library

Created by Oracle Experts
FREE for Oracle Users

✓ Vast array of learning aids

✓ Intuitive & powerful search

✓ Share content, events & saved searches

✓ Personalize your learning dashboard

✓ Find & register for training events